FALSE FLAG 911

How Bush, Cheney and the Saudis Created the Post-911 World

PHILIP MARSHALL

pilotsof911@aol.com

Copyright © 2008 by Philip Marshall
All rights reserved.

For information, please contact:
pilotsof911@aol.com

Excerpts from "The Dirtiest Bank of All" © 1991 by Time Inc.
Used by permission.

Cover design by Laura Owen Sutherland
Text design by William Van Doren

ISBN-13: 978-1-4392-0264-8
ISBN-10: 1-4392-0264-8

2008906140

To Jon Stewart of The Daily Show — seriously — for rescuing freedom of speech with humor and, an oddity on commercial television, real facts. And for getting it mostly right — on the comedy channel! Many days during the writing of this book I was beaten down and without hope, and that one light would shine through. He's done more than anyone to stand up and say, "I'm an American, and I don't need to be afraid."

ACKNOWLEDGMENTS

Thanks to my editor, Bill Van Doren, for his tireless efforts to pull me out of the mud, keep this locomotive on the rails and generally fix mixed-up expressions like this one, and more. Bill not only counseled me as an editor but pushed me on everything, until I was forced to make the picture crystal clear. My deep appreciation to a master writer and all-around good guy.

Preface

On September 11, 2001, I watched with a mix of horrified shock and uneasy suspicion as the attack changed the world on live television. From day one, I listened closely and collected articles and other materials. Beginning in 2005, I began to research all that had been collected, with little idea where it would lead. The guilt needle soon began pointing in one steady direction. Three years later that needle has yet to waver.

From 1989 until 2005, I was a pilot for one of the airlines whose planes were hijacked on 911, flying throughout the world exclusively on Boeing aircraft. I had earned my captain ratings on the 727, 737, 747, 747-400 and, most importantly for this book, the Boeing 757 and 767, the very planes used by the 911 Raiders. I knew both Captain Jason Dahl of United 93 and Captain Vic Saracini of United 175. I had flown with most of the flight attendants who perished on that day.

Even if I'd had no other reason to investigate, my airline family deserved an honest account of the attack. I might add that we also deserve this because 911 has been used against us ever since, in a running nightmare of contrived bankruptcy, draconian working conditions and hostile management.

I have circled the world with the dedicated employees of our company on thousands of domestic and international routes. Together we've hit nearly every commercial runway within the United States, with dozens of entries into each of the three airports used on 911, and in nearly every major city of the world. In 2003, we flew 747 charters for the U.S. military, delivering young Marines to the battlefield via Kuwait. During this period, I wrote my first book, *Lakefront Airport*, based on my experiences as a covert player during the 1980s for the first Bush Administration. This inside criminal operation became known as Iran Contra. Alarmingly, major covert players from Iran-Contra resurfaced in the 911 evidence. In aviation training, we call this kind of thing a red flag. The covert activities — "black operations" or black ops — I witnessed during the first Bush administration seem to have laid the groundwork for unthinkable black ops in the second.

My experience in government-sponsored covert operations provides insight into how black ops, such as the activities of Blackwater and other private contractors, work. My experience as a Boeing captain contributes a clear picture of aviation-related aspects of 911 that have remained obscure for the general public. I also worked for years in and around the oil industry — as a roughneck on rigs in the Gulf of Mexico in the late 1970s, and flying Learjet charters for Halliburton and other oil-related companies from my hometown of New Orleans and later out of Dallas in the early 1980s. Oil, aviation and covert operations: these are three major areas in the world of 911.

The 911 Commission Report, distorted largely through the efforts of its White House–appointed executive director Philip Zelikow, fails to provide an accurate timeline for the attack. By placing events out of chronological order, the report tends to confuse readers. Descriptions of the attack here have been placed in chronological order using FAA records, radar records, NTSB reports, 911 Commission research, cockpit voice recordings, testimony from air traffic controllers, American and United airlines dispatchers and other official records. Except for the flying analysis, the hard evidence in this book has been compiled by others: by congressional investigators, 911 Commission investigators, FBI, FAA and NTSB investigators, and by the authors of published reports in major world newspapers and magazines. I cite several nonfiction books as background and for cross-reference and I highly recommend each of them.

My research into 911 raised many red flags, but ultimately pointed to a type of covert operation, used time and time again in history, known as a "false flag."

A false flag is defined as an act of aggression meant to appear as though it was carried out by your enemies.

— *Philip Marshall*

Introduction:
911 as Executed, 911 as Planned

After any tactical operation is completed, its plan becomes evident. The work of the Raiders on September 11th, 2001, shows that the element of surprise allowed the first wave of attack against New York to go unchallenged. But then the advantage of surprise was lost, and at that point, given that this was a multipronged attack involving several airliners, every second of delay jeopardized the rest of the mission. Although time is important in any tactical plan, time — Time with a capital T — was mission-critical for the Raiders. On 911, the delay between the New York attacks and the strike on the Pentagon, followed by the crash of United 93 in Pennsylvania, meant that although they achieved spectacular tactical successes, in strategic terms the Raiders actually failed.

Almost all attention concerning 911 has been focused on the terrible deeds that the Raiders accomplished. However, it is at least as important to focus on what they did not accomplish — how the attack was *intended* to unfold, and what it was designed to achieve. Those are the terms in which the Raiders failed, and that failure may eventually prove to be their undoing.

The Raiders chose four perfect flights to hijack. All were scheduled to depart within minutes of each other from three separate airports. All were among the first flights of the morning, and therefore among the least likely to be delayed. Because of unpredictable taxi times at these busy airports, it would be hard to know which plane would hit its target first. But if things went just right, they might have all hit within minutes if not seconds of each other.

All four airplanes were fully fueled and loaded and pushed back from their gates on schedule. American 11 pushed back from the gate at Boston at 7:50. United 175 pushed back, also from Boston, at 7:59. United 93 pushed back from Newark at 8:01 and American 77 pushed back from Dulles at 8:10.

At this point, the odds were excellent that all four airplanes would be airborne by 8:15, all would reach their windows for takeover by 8:40 and all would soon be burning within their targets. By 9:11, interestingly enough, Americans would be witnessing something that would look very much like Armageddon.

What actually happened was horrific enough. But consider the impact of nearly *simultaneous* strikes on the World Trade Center and the Pentagon *and* the destruction of the Capitol dome. This was the plan: fire and brimstone killing thousands of Americans on live television, along with the decapitation of the best-known symbol of the republic. As profound as the psychological impact of 911 has been, the trauma of what was intended to happen would have ratcheted that impact up to a level that is difficult to conceive or calculate, except to say that it would be capable of producing almost unlimited political consequences, and for a very long time.

Had the plan gone as designed, the Raiders could expect a frantic but fruitless response from the U.S. defenses. By 9:11, Americans would be in a state of profound shock and even real terror. The President of the United States would give a somber speech from an elementary school where he had been showing compassion for America's students, reading an innocent story to seven-year-olds. It would be obvious that there hadn't been a damn thing he could do, after immediately launching waves of fighter jets from Cape Cod to Dover to Maryland to Hampton Roads, only to find that the sneak attack had long been completed and nothing but smoke filled the skies. He would soon identify the evildoers and bravely send the American military into a new era of retaliation.

But it didn't happen that way. When the tactical plan is analyzed in aviation terms, it becomes clear that the hijackers did not just fail by not managing to crash United 93 into the Capitol dome, they failed to achieve one of the most important goals of the overall mission. They failed because it is the delays, the long duration of the four hijackings, that tends to expose the identity of the real Raiders — meaning not the nominal hijackers but the mission planners and architects. The actions, and the inaction, of a small number of key individuals within the Executive Branch before and after the attacks were remarkable. But it is their behavior during the rather extended period of the nightmare of 911 that will ultimately serve to bring the perpetrators to light, if not to justice.

1

If any airliner is hijacked and the FAA's Air Traffic Control knows it, ATC's first call will be to the North American Aerospace Defense Command. NORAD would immediately dispatch jet fighters to intercept and the President's National Security Advisor would be notified. From there, the fighters would monitor the airliners' intentions and a shootdown order could be given by the President.

There were four separate but coordinated attack plans. American 11, a Boeing 767 bound from Boston to Los Angeles, was hijacked first and was crashed into the north tower of the World Trade Center. United 175, also a Boeing 767, also departed Boston for LAX and was hijacked over New Jersey just as AA11 impacted its target and would hit the south tower just 14 minutes later. American 77, a Boeing 757, departed from Washington Dulles for Los Angeles and was hijacked 33 minutes after takeoff, reversed course, and impacted the Pentagon 40 minutes later without meeting any interference.

United 93 from Newark to San Francisco encountered two intangibles that caused the only complete failure among the Raiders' four plans. The flight was delayed for forty minutes taxiing out to the end of the runway, and then the cockpit takeover was 30 minutes late, leaving the aircraft over 270 miles from its target when it was finally commandeered.

For an airliner at cruise altitude commandeered for use as a guided missile, ideal attack position does not mean a location directly over the target. The best attack position for an aircraft at 35,000 feet is somewhere within 120 miles of the target. Because airliners require three horizontal miles to descend each 1,000 feet, pilots plan a descent from 35,000 feet at around 105 miles from the destination. The 3 to 1 ratio can be increased to 2 to 1 for a more aggressive descent using spoilers and higher airspeeds, but the pass/fail of the hijackers' mission depended on the ability to commandeer all the aircraft within a critical 120-mile window.

Getting the four scheduled airliners into an ideal strike position, as close as possible to the same moment, was perhaps the most challenging aspect of the plan. Drawing 120-mile circles around New York and Washington shows the windows that the planes needed to be within for success. Based on the departure airports and the targets hit, it is clear that all four flights were planned to be within ideal position soon after takeoff. Any delay in the hostile takeovers would open a new can of worms. Most importantly, the U.S. military's blanket of supersonic fighters would begin to defend American skies.

AA11 was commandeered only 15 minutes after takeoff and was in perfect attack position at 8:14 A.M. UA175 was commandeered 33 minutes after liftoff and was in an ideal attack position at 8:46 A.M., just as AA11 struck the north tower.

The snapshot at 8:46 shows AA11 about to hit the north tower and, in perfect synchrony, the attackers storming the cockpit of UA175. AA77 — the Pentagon plane — was heading west at cruise altitude, moving away from its target at 500 mph, and still five minutes from takeover. The hijackers on UA93 had lifted off only four minutes earlier from Newark, after a 40-minute taxi out and delay due to normal traffic. They came extremely close to missing their first critical time window, but the window was met, if only by four minutes.

Long taxi outs from busy airports are hard to predict. The UA93 attack was in jeopardy before liftoff because of the long taxi time. Getting an early pushback away from the gate by the ground crew can make a huge difference in the placement for takeoff. There are many scheduled departures around 8:00 A.M. from all major airports. If you're first in pushing back, your taxi time will be minimal. But if you don't call for pushback until, perhaps, 8:02, there might be 15 airplanes getting into position ahead of you. Each takeoff takes an average of three minutes, so 15 airplanes equals around 45 minutes. So it appears that UA93 was somewhere around number 12 in line for takeoff — completely normal, but not good for the tactical plan.

This long taxi nearly busted one of the tactical plan's critical windows. The goal was to have all four airplanes in the air and in attack position before ATC or NORAD knew what was happening. Preserving the element of surprise requires calculating the amount of time it will take for the system to switch from a normal operating day to a day in which there is one odd occurrence to a day with one emergency to the realization that the country is under attack. A further delay for UA93 of just four minutes would have blown their critical time window, because the controllers and even United 93's pilots would have seen the World Trade Center on fire with their own eyes, from the ground at Newark Airport.

2

As a Boeing 757 and 767 captain — on one of the airlines and the same aircraft used on September 11, 2001 — I had both professional and personal reasons to seek a complete understanding of the attacks. I hoped to find some reassurance. That's not what I got.

I had heard wild theories about missiles fired into the Pentagon as part of a government conspiracy and another about explosives planted to take down the towers of the World Trade Center. These theories, which hinged in part on the idea that airliners could not have caused the kind of destruction seen that day, were offered by people with no background in aviation or aerospace engineering but were nevertheless given considerable press coverage.

It was easy enough to disprove the theories about missiles and explosives. The missile into the Pentagon theory couldn't be supported. I obtained radar images of the track of American 77. The NTSB report was accurate and eyewitness reports accounted for the missing Boeing 757. The NTSB and FBI recovered the entire aircraft, which had slammed the building at over 500 miles per hour and there is a mountain of credible documentation. The image of the aircraft captured on a security camera in the Pentagon's parking lot showed the 757 a few feet off the ground just before impact.

The missile confusion is understandable because of the speed of AA77 as it dove toward the Pentagon. The official NTSB report reveals that the aircraft made an incredible hit at 480 knots, or 540 miles per hour, which *is* missile speed and would produce a missile sound. Washingtonians are accustomed to seeing aircraft at the normal speed of around 150 m.p.h. on approaches into National Airport as airliners are speed restricted and slowing for landing. But it was precisely this phenomenal speed that began to show me that these hijackers were better trained than first thought, and was one of the first pieces of evidence that brought up the question: Who trained these guys? As a 20-year veteran airline pilot, I know that hitting a 90-foot target with a 757 at 500 miles per hour is extremely difficult — absolutely impossible for first-time flyers of a heavy airliner. It's like seeing Tiger Woods hit a 300-yard 1 iron and someone telling you he'd never practiced the shot.

As for the Twin Towers collapse, both Boeing 767s that were used (strategically, it turns out) were carrying around 12,000 gallons of flammable jet fuel when they impacted at 545 miles per hour. This incredible airspeed, twice the normal operating speed, reveals that these pilots had been well trained and comfortable in pushing the plane above the published maximum airspeed limits. There was catastrophic damage to the towers' steel structure by the impact of the 250,000-pound aircraft and the annihilation was made complete by the ignited jet fuel, which cascaded from the impact site, around 800 feet up, to ground zero. Jet fuel was the accelerant that ignited all combustible items, which raised the temperature enough within an hour to weaken the steel framework. The forces of gravity finished the job. The adjacent World Trade Center Building 7 collapsed as a result of two 101-story columns of steel, glass, brick and mortar, along with desks, generators, plumbing and the wreckage of two Boeing 767s crashing into the ground, blowing out windows and igniting the building in a thunderous fireball. Building 7 was engulfed in flame for eight hours before it finally collapsed.

These findings invalidated theories about missiles and planted explosives. But I couldn't help noticing key aspects of the attacks that were not accounted for in the officially accepted story of a straightforward terrorist mission.

Among many discrepancies, the most striking was one that perhaps only professional pilots would notice. Except for serious and understandable errors in the piloting of United 93, there was the remarkably high level of airmanship required to execute these attacks. The more I delved into the details, the clearer it became that the flying ability required for these strikes could not have been achieved, as the official record maintains, by novice pilots with the minimal number of training hours they were supposed to have spent on computer games and outdated simulators and in small, single-engine airplanes.

Once this discrepancy appeared and refused to go away, other questions surfaced. If the hijacker pilots could not have flown this well with the training we had heard about, then how did they do it? How did they learn to fly and execute advanced maneuvers that would have been dangerous even under normal, peaceful conditions? How could they have been trained? Where? By whom?

In addition to their control of the aircraft, there was the problem of the attackers' execution of a coordinated plan that depended on subtle and intricate knowledge of the ATC system and U.S. defenses at a very high level. It would be preposterous to conclude that foreign, novice pilots executed these plans and had known all that they needed to know without expert help. Suspicions only multiplied with the odd responses of the Executive Branch before, during and after that day. The actions of the U.S. administration on nearly every front only served to generate more questions.

3

For the Raiders, the alligator closest to the boat would be the fighter jets based around the United States. Along the Northeast corridor between Boston and New York, Otis Air Force Base on Cape Cod would be the place where F-15 fighters would be dispatched to intercept and shoot down any airliner that had been converted into a guided missile. Washington, D.C., was trickier for the hijackers, with two close Air Force bases: Andrews right outside of town and Langley just to the south, at Hampton, Virginia. As in all sneak attacks, any confusion (such as among air traffic controllers) and any indecision (such as by government officials) would work to the benefit of the Raiders. If there were any official failures to recognize and respond, the attackers would coin them into pure minutes and seconds: time — precious Time. A key for the Raiders was that none of the fighter jets would matter if the tactical plan was executed with perfection. Only mistakes by the Raiders would give the fighters a chance to do their job.

America is defended by trillions of dollars' worth of arsenal. The most challenging aspect of conducting an air raid against the United States is that, with the help of a secure blanket of radar coverage, the nation is constantly protected by the world's most advanced system of military fighter jets. These fighters are ready to scramble at a moment's notice with a variety of lethal missiles capable of taking down any hostile aircraft in short order. Fighter pilots sleep and eat within minutes of their jets and have drilled to be airborne within seconds of an all-out scramble. This constant readiness is paramount in the nation's defense.

The normal life expectancy for a hostile aircraft anywhere within U.S. borders is less than 30 minutes. But the hard evidence is that on 911, hostile aircraft were able to operate for nearly two hours. It should be disturbing to any American taxpayer that a full inquiry into this failure has yet to be accomplished.

If the President of the United States is still breathing, he and only he is authorized to convert a fighter jet scramble to a shoot-down of threatening aircraft, the order going, via a strict protocol, to the Secretary of Defense to the Combatant Commander to the fighter pilots. In the world of commercial aviation alone, we have progressed to a point of nearly perfect, nearly instant communication. Communications among the FAA, White House and U.S. military are even better. In the real world of the year 2001, the protocol for a shootdown order to go through the chain of command would be expected to require less than a minute.

But if the protocol is never initiated, then the trillions of dollars in weaponry are worthless. No fighter pilot is going to be shooting down any airplane, especially a commercial airliner in domestic air space, without shootdown orders.

4

The focus of my research shifted from the theorized explosives to the real planning and execution of the mission. It became evident that this attack was planned with the help of a highly experienced technical support team. Although imperfectly executed, the tactical plan to defeat the world's most sophisticated defense was flawless, potentially leaving all of our jet fighters, radar sites and missiles useless. The planning, knowledge and skill required for the mission involved a host of matters large and small, basic and highly esoteric. Somehow the hijackers had confidence that they could defeat airline security with lethal weapons that would just narrowly pass checkpoint scrutiny — as if this matter had been thoroughly tested. The flying of the highly complex Boeing aircraft, in three out of the four cases, was phenomenal, as we will explore in detail. The execution of the attack called for the precise coordination of four scheduled and on-time airline departures, a major challenge in itself. The coordinated flights were planned to be hijacked in a narrow time frame without delay and the pilot/hijackers had to know their exact location in the air at the time of a murderous, bloody and chaotic takeover. The planning was designed to place the airplanes in attack position nearly simultaneously.

After the bloody takeovers, the Boeing cockpits were swiftly and expertly transitioned from a climb and cruise mode to a screaming descent. Flight path recordings indicate immediate turns to the perfect courses, and the descent profiles were flown expertly. American 77 flawlessly completed a difficult low-altitude 330-degree turn before it torpedoed the Pentagon just three feet off the ground at 540 miles per hour. United 175 was taken from cruise mode into a hair-raising descent, slamming the south tower just five minutes after leaving 31,000 feet. The hijackers flew at expert levels of airmanship on airliners that require a six-week training course — *for experienced airline pilots* — *and* did it single-pilot, without an experienced copilot, in a large cockpit designed for two professional aviators.

5

To illustrate the aviation challenges faced by the hijackers, consider the one case in which they failed completely. This is the story of Ziad Jarrah at the controls of United 93.

When United 93 departed Newark, 179 miles from Washington, the Boeing 757 climbed out within a huge high pressure area. Captain Jason Dahl made an announcement to the passengers about the flight to California, giving the planned route and the weather forecast for San Francisco; he asked the passengers to relax and enjoy the flight and he switched the seat belt signs off.

Because Washington is southwest of Newark, the 757 was flying along the northern portion of the 120-mile radius that defined the tactical plan's ideal attack window. Just as they reached the cruise altitude of 35,000 feet, they were only 112 miles due north of the Capitol building — prime position for the hijackers to begin the assault. At the top of his climb, Captain Dahl set cruise speed at .82 Mach; now the twin jet engines were pushing the plane away from its target at 510 miles per hour.

United Airlines flight attendants follow a routine on transcontinental flights that is rarely modified. I recently had seat 1B, in the first row of first class, on the aisle on a United transcontinental flight. This is where Ziad Jarrah had sat on United 93.

It was easy enough to visualize how things might have started out on that day in 2001. Perhaps the New York–based flight attendants could be overheard chatting, on the taxi out, discussing everyday concerns such as barely meeting rents on modest apartments and modest New York lifestyles. They would have been busy about their work, treating all the passengers, Muslim and Christian and Jew, with respect and dignity, not knowing or caring which belief came with which body.

As the 757 reached its cruise altitude 20 minutes after takeoff, an attendant would have handed each passenger a steaming hot towel as breakfast wafted from the forward galley. Another attendant would be pouring mimosas and checking to make sure tablecloths were in place. They were probably smiling and just doing their jobs, quite unaware of political differences and injustices around the world.

"Good morning, sir, may I offer you some champagne?"

Handing out a menu: "Is there anything here that catches your fancy? We have omelets, fruit plates, and you know, the chef has cooked up a special for the California flights . . . ."

Perhaps in this situation Ziad Jarrah was catching a warm fuzzy feeling with all the smiles and the service, plus the satisfaction of knowing that he had learned so much about this very complicated jet that was now pushing westbound past his critical takeover point. Perhaps he was anxious; perhaps it just didn't feel right to kill all of these innocent people. Whatever he may have been thinking, it is clear that he was not executing the tactical plan.

Ziad Jarrah had learned only parts of the technology that had produced the awesome airliner that was flying so smoothly, a technological masterpiece with sophisticated fuel, electrical and hydraulic systems that he didn't fully understand. But he surely knew that the so-called automatic pilot was damned complicated. In fact, he knew that pushing the wrong button at the wrong time would create a nightmare of confusion. He had become familiar with the flight management computer and may even have heard the United pilots programming the FMC before the cockpit door closed at Newark. He knew something about the all-important Flitch button and the vertical speed selector within the complicated panel on the glareshield. He knew that the autopilot was useless unless it was getting reliable information on which to navigate. He knew that there is nothing automatic about operating the autopilot.

Jarrah had surely discovered what every last airline pilot knows, which is that reading the 1,000-page flight manual of this or any other airliner leads only to confusion. None of it makes sense until you actually get your hands on the yoke, to get the feel, to see what happens when you actually touch the Flight Level Change or "Flitch" button and the engines go to full power and the button does exactly the *opposite* of what you thought it might do. But . . . I wanted to go down, not up! I wanted to go left, not right! The airplane is unforgiving and insensitive, yelling at the pilots with red flashing lights, buzzers, beeps, clicking noises, bells, voices yelling "PULL UP, PULL UP, GLIDESLOPE, TRAFFIC . . . TRAFFIC . . . DESCEND . . . CLIMB . . . TOO LOW, TOO FAST, TOO whatever . . . ." with each and every mistake.

The cockpit is off-limits to passengers and even to flight attendants during critical phases of flight because mistakes on takeoff and landing have historically resulted in tragedy. Because we keep the world out of the cockpit during these times, the public is left with a dramatic but distorted Hollywood image of fictional characters playing at being a pilot. Dozens of movies have combined to create a false and truly crazy picture of what it takes to fly a commercial airliner. We've all seen the frightened flight attendant flying a 747 with the front windshield blown out, and her hair hardly moves although the wind would be blasting through at 400 knots. I saw Kurt Russell play a passenger who takes the controls of a one million–pound 747 and lands it just by putting the landing gear down, licking his lips and slamming on the brakes. The realities of physics don't come into play in a movie script. But the realities can be seen in the final moments of United 93: a huge orange fireball and a crater 12 feet deep.

The reality of flying makes a stark contrast not only with the Hollywood fiction, but with the strange assumption that the hijackers could have flown as they did with the training they were said to have received. The reality is that each U.S. airline has a high-tech flight training center. The reality is that Boeing 757 captains rely heavily on highly trained copilots, and together they work as a single four-armed unit, setting and rechecking navigation frequencies, confirming altitudes, confirming flight director commands and conducting each flight within strict Standard Operating Procedures. Once pilots leave the paved road of SOP, they find themselves in the trees very quickly. If you ever get behind the two-man cockpit, you better damn well know what to do, and fast, before all hell breaks loose.

The reality is that for experienced line pilots, including 20-year veteran Boeing captains, just to transition to the 767 requires two grueling months at the training center. About a month before training starts, the thousand-page manual arrives in the mail. It is expected that the pilot read and understand the entire manual before he arrives for school. Even after a month of pre-study, there is a two week "ground school" on the material, followed by a written exam. Each complex system needs to be completely understood before a pilot proceeds to the next phase of training, to a cockpit procedures trainer or CPT.

For two weeks within a simulated cockpit, pilots learn to work as a team, programming the Flight Management Computer and learning all the procedures of vertical and horizontal navigation, power settings and the hand-eye coordination required to get two dozen switches in the proper positions so that the "autopilot" won't kill you — and the 300 souls behind you.

Once past another four-hour test on these procedures, it's on to the simulator for three more weeks of engine failures, fires, hydraulic blowouts, electrical malfunctions and an assortment of other irregular operations. The full motion simulator moves around on hydraulic lifts to simulate gravity forces, which coincide with the visual simulation of images where the windshield would be. At the end of an intense course of training sessions the pilot is taken into a briefing room for a one-on-one oral exam with an FAA inspector. Nothing is off limits for the examiner as he turns to any of the pages of the flight manual or any of the 800 pages of federal regulations or company operating procedures. If the pilot survives the oral, it's back to the simulator for another four hours of emergency and normal procedures testing before he is allowed to leave the training center. If the pilot survives the final testing, and many do not, he is allowed to return to the line as if released from Angola, usually with a bruised ego. But the training is still not over as he enters the next stage as if on parole.

The next two weeks is flying with an aircraft training officer who watches the new pilot's every move until he proves worthy to perform required duties. After he is signed off, the crew schedulers are required to give the new pilot an experienced 767 pilot for the next 100 hours on the line. And with 14 transition trainings under my belt, I can testify that no pilot is completely comfortable for many months on his new flying machine.

The reality is that for heavy complicated airliners, there are no specially gifted aviators of the last generation who could just fly from the seat of their pants and simply think their way out of trouble. Intense flight training is the only way to learn the avionics codes and the feel of a heavy Boeing 767. If you were to find yourself tasked with giving a crash course to teach suicidal maniacs how to take the plane from altitude to a kamikaze mission, it would be virtually impossible without a highly experienced instructor using an actual Boeing 767. Because the 911 hijackers were novice and Arabic was their first language, it would be absolutely imperative that their instructors also speak Arabic. There would be no room for linguistic misunderstandings and no room for errors. The mission would have to be practiced, time and time again — someone would need to make damn sure these hijackers could fly the actual airplanes — if they were going to find success, if they were going to change the world in one horrific hour.

My search began for an entity or group who could have met all the requirements for training these hijackers. Few suspects would fit the three hard requirements: the opportunity to access actual Boeing 757s and 767s, an experienced Arab-speaking Boeing instructor and an airport from which to operate the many training flights that would be needed. Once I identified just such an entity or combination of entities, many 911 mysteries began to fall like dominos.

Perhaps Ziad Jarrah was scared and trying to remember all the things he had been trained to do as United 93 exited the ideal strike position: First he and the three muscle guys must kill these flight attendants who were treating him so well, break into the cockpit, kill the pilots, pull them from their seats, let the muscle guys handle the passengers with box cutters, threats, fake bombs and murder, while he jumped into the captain's seat to turn off the transponder, turn the airplane to the target, dial in the correct frequencies, set the altitude selector to 10,000 feet, the vertical speed knob to minus 4,000, the heading select to 120, make an announcement to the passengers, disarm the overspeed warnings and Ground Proximity Warning System, track inbound to the localizer at Washington National, spot the Capitol, disconnect the autopilot, push up the throttles and hand fly the plane into a suicide dive.

Perhaps it just didn't seem right, to ruin this nice airplane, to kill this pretty flight attendant and to spoil a wonderful first-class breakfast as United 93 clicked away from its closest point to the Capitol building — at 112 miles — to 120 miles — to 140 — to 160, 180, 200, 250 and past 270 miles, in the next 32 minutes.

Luckily for America, the occupants of the Capitol Building and eventually the seekers of truth, the murderous assault on the surprised crew was delayed until 42 minutes after takeoff, and by the time the cockpit was under the hijackers' control at 9:32, Jarrah's ETA for his target was now 10:12, an hour over the tactical plan. His tardiness presented another major problem: Those supersonic fighters based at Andrews and Langley and Dover had abundant time to scramble and defend the skies over his target in Washington. In fact, by 10:00, the entire world was aware of what was taking place. The element of surprise was gone and with the communication capabilities of 2001, even the passengers in the back understood what he intended to do.

Recovered from the crater at the crash site was United 93's flight data recorder. It tells investigators what Ziad Jarrah did with the autopilot and why he missed the Capitol building by 114 miles. Instead of clearing what Captain Dahl had programmed on the flight management control panel at the originally planned time — 25 minutes after takeoff — he didn't get this done until 52 minutes after takeoff, and 170 miles off the tactical plan. Someone had trained him to reset the FMC using a non-standard method, which indicates that he received this information somewhere other than the Boeing flight manual. He immediately set his target altitude to 10,000 feet and changed the autopilot from the normal cruise mode to a vertical (up or down) speed mode, which overrides the altitude selected for the autopilot. We can see from the flight data recorder that he mistakenly set the vertical speed selector to a rate of 1,800 feet a minute up — instead of 4,000 feet a minute down. His altitude setting to 10,000 feet was nullified. The fuel flow readings confirm this mistake. The engines powered up, the plane began a slow but steady climb and would soon teeter on a stall as it climbed above 40,000 feet and warnings began to sound and the yoke began to shake. There was no gauge to record Jarrah's heart rate, but I'm sure it was in the red zone too, after he had helped kill Jason Dahl and his first officer, bleeding to death on the floor behind him, and now realized he was in no man's land — behind the power curve in a dark blue sky and still 265 miles from his target.

At 40,000 the airplane was barely flying because of the thin atmosphere and the weight of the plane. Jarrah had about 10 seconds to discover his mistake before the aircraft would stall; once the plane stalls and breaks into a spin, it's all over but the crying. The cockpit warning would have been a "stick shaker" that alerts the pilot to an impending stall. Both the captain's and copilot's yokes have motors that shake them — the last warning before the plane falls out of the sky. Just seconds before the stall, Jarrah luckily found his error and re-set the vertical speed to 4,000 feet down and the aircraft slowly recovered speed and began descending to 10,000 feet.

But then he slipped up again. He began to execute the flight plan as if he had not waited too long and was back in the window. He tried to tune the radios to National Airport, which would have worked 100 miles earlier but he was now too far away to receive. In layman's terms, he was screwed. Because he waited too long, the passengers were getting information about the attacks on New York and knew they needed to get these guys.

As Jarrah descended into the unknown, it became obvious that he had missed his window and needed to revert to plan B, ending it before the passengers got them. Maybe a deadheading pilot or even Kurt Russell himself was on board to fly the plane if the passengers took over.

In Arabic: "Should we finish it?" The cockpit voice recorder reveals that the passengers were slamming the beverage cart into the cockpit door as Jarrah disconnected the autopilot with chants of "God is great!" and rolled the 757 on its back. Recorded airspeed began increasing to 300, 350, 400, 450, 500 and the vertical speed rate was pegged out at over 30,000 feet per minute at impact, 114 miles from the capital.

United 93 was the only plane that missed its target. If Jarrah had taken control at the ideal time, United 93 would have crushed the Capitol dome at 9:11.

6

This mission with novice, native Arabic-speaking pilots was virtually impossible without repeated intensive training flights in actual Boeing aircraft with experienced, Arabic-speaking Boeing instructors. For example, the advanced maneuvers that were the cornerstone of the attacks are not described in any published training materials. Unhooking the autopilot at high altitude requires serious practice and mistakes on pitch control would result in either a high- or low-speed stall which, for novice pilots, is unrecoverable. Beyond this, complicated systems needed to be located and disarmed — immediately — in order to fly the airplanes in the abnormal and reckless ways demonstrated on that day. This would have required a Boeing expert to anticipate the ramifications of flying at over three times the normal descent rates and airspeeds well beyond the red line at low altitude.

The 911 raiders demonstrated an intricate knowledge both of the systems they commandeered and the systems they defeated. They would have needed to understand the locations and reaction times of the dozens of available quick-response military fighter bases, radars and missile defense systems strategically set up in the Northeast and around Washington. The tactical planners displayed an advanced understanding on every front, even in the choice of airliners to hijack. They selected planes with the fuel load that would be required to demolish the World Trade Center towers, differentiating them from the planes used to torpedo the side of the Pentagon or destroy the relatively small and fragile Capitol Building. The flight plans for the 767s flying out to Los Angeles from Boston called for five hours of flight time, which required nearly 12,000 gallons of flammable jet fuel to be loaded into the wings and lower fuselage. If 757s had been used on the Trade Center, the results would have been less damaging. Although the planes are generally similar, the fuel capacity of a 767 is double that of the 757.

7

Before any commercial airliner is dispatched for flight, primary and backup electronic transponders must be operational. The transponders are a major part of the air traffic control system, relaying an electronic signal, recognized by ATC radar, that transmits all the pertinent flight information — flight number, type of aircraft, groundspeed, altitude, cleared route, departure airport and destination — in one easy-to-read block on the controller's screen. The 911 hijackers were keenly aware of this obscure feature. The transponder's role in the system is a subtle piece of information that pilots hardly notice as they plow through the 767's manual. But the pilot/hijackers had been specifically trained to turn the transponders off immediately after commandeering the craft, a move that was designed to create initial confusion in a deadly game of hide and seek against the ATC and military defense systems.

Based on expected routine radio calls to ATC that never came from the two murdered pilots, we know that AA11 was hijacked at 8:14 A.M. As in all four attacks, evidence indicates that the cockpit was stormed, the pilots were killed with boxcutters and the passengers were herded to the back of the plane under direct force, mace, bomb threats, bloodshed and panic. The hijackers knew that the autopilot would be engaged, so they could rip the pilots out of their seats without losing control of the craft. There was one pilot on each hijacker team of five (or four, in the case of United 93); the remaining four (or three) were muscle guys. Evidence indicates that each plane was under the hijackers' control within ten minutes after the cockpit was stormed.

In the case of AA11, by 8:21 Mohamed Atta was in the captain seat and in control of the aircraft. We know this because, at 8:21, just before the Boeing 767 turned south on a course for New York, the transponder was switched off and ATC instantly lost AA11's data on their radar screens. There was still a simple or "primary" radar return, but it was one among dozens. No one was expecting the airplane to deviate from its cleared route over the vicinity of Albany, and make a screaming beeline for the World Trade Center.

8

In the American mind, if one thing's for certain, it is that Osama bin Laden, the elusive, shady, evil creature, is responsible for the 911 attacks. We know this because every day for the past seven years, this conclusion has been reported and repeated by the trusted media and has become "common knowledge" in the American conversation.

Innocent until proven guilty was a tenet of the Pre-911 America. In the Post-911 World, convicting suspects without a trial or without so much as listening to the statements of the accused has become normal. Justice itself has been hijacked and crashed in media trials without oath and without testimony.

A visit to bin Laden's poster on the FBI's website tells an interesting story. This will be hard to fathom and I hope you're sitting down, but the FBI poster suggests that perhaps the Bush Administration hasn't been completely honest in their accounts of the hunt for Osama bin Laden.

Within the FBI's Most Wanted Terrorist List, sure enough, we find the color picture of the lanky olive-skinned Saudi Arabian with white turban, his acts of terrorism clearly listed. He's wanted in connection with the August 7, 1998 bombings of the United States Embassies in Dar es Salaam, Tanzania, and Nairobi, Kenya, and of course he's wanted for — hey, wait a second! There's not one mention of the September 11, 2001 attacks! How can this be?

Haven't we all seen his 2004 "confession" videos on national broadcasts and the interpreted transcripts published in every major newspaper? Two-minute segments of these tapes were analyzed by none other than the experts at NBC News, Fox and CNN. We all know, therefore, beyond a reasonable doubt, that it is bin Laden who runs the terrorist world and who planned and executed 911, even though almost no one among us can decipher a single word the man has said. And even though there has been no accounting or explanation — not one — of how he was actually able to plan 911 and defeat the U.S. military, America has convicted him. A verdict has been reached on the greatest criminal act in American history without evidence, testimony, trial or jury.

The FBI's profile of Osama bin Laden states that he is a 6'4" to 6'6", weighs approximately 160 pounds, is left handed and walks with a cane. A close look at the "confession" video, released five days before the 2004 presidential election (the "October surprise"), shows the image of a composed man reading a speech for the media, dressed in a gold robe and a familiar white turban, holding the typed speech in his hands as if he had transformed into a news anchor. His beard is gray and he is casually fingering the pages with . . . his right hand? — although his left hand appears to move normally. A closer look indicates that his hands are smaller and less rugged than known pictures of bin Laden and his nose is wider and flatter than known pictures and — hey! This isn't bin Laden at all!

In addition, transcriptions of the vague "confession" videos have "bin Laden" saying things about the operation that we know aren't true.

Another video released just days before the sixth anniversary of 911 shows yet *another,* darker skinned man. This time his beard is completely black and his head is smaller than the 2004 version. NBC News used the video to lead off its broadcast of September 7, 2007. A concerned Brian Williams asks the correspondent covering the story about the "obvious change to his [bin Laden's] physical bearing." The correspondent agrees that it is quite puzzling before quipping, I kid you not, "It's Osama bin Laden the pundit." An unknown interpreter tells us that bin Laden is questioning the newly elected Democrats in Congress, although the reporter says that for over half of the video the picture was frozen. The correspondent concludes the media fantasy: "And just before we went on the air, Brian, a senior administration official confirmed, that it really is him."

And this is all it takes for millions of us to believe that it really is him. Americans have been led to believe that Osama bin Laden is hiding out in a cave and painting Hair Color for Men on his beard before delivering commentary on Democrats. The first phony bin Laden appeared in late 2001 and after highly technical testing comparing previous bin Laden recordings, the respected lab Dalle Molle Institute for Perceptual Artificial Intelligence based in Lausanne, Switzerland, announced their finding that . . . it really *isn't* him. Arab experts laugh at the prospect of an Arab man dying the gray, a sign of wisdom and integrity, from his beard. Another Arab expert stated that the phony bin Laden was 40 to 50 pounds heavier than the reported 160-pounder that the FBI poster describes. These reports on the 2001, 2004 and 2007 videos never made it to the NBC Nightly News.

Further investigation brings new light. Almost entirely unreported in the U.S. was that Osama bin Laden, interviewed on September 28, 2001 for the national Pakistani paper *Ummat*, denied any involvement in the 911 attacks. Is that any way for a terrorist to behave? The world leader of jihad declines to take credit for defeating the world's greatest military on its own turf?

"I have already said that I am not involved in the 11 September attacks in the United States. I had no knowledge of these attacks, nor do I consider the killing of innocent women, children and other humans as an appreciable act." This interview was hardly mentioned in the American media. He confirmed his anger toward the United States military and Saudi infidels who support America, but steadfastly denied complicity in the attacks.

Also scarce in the American media were the published obituaries from the Pakistani *Observer* and the Egyptian paper *Ad-Wafd* on December 26, 2001: According to funeral witnesses, bin Laden had died of kidney failure on December 14, 2001, and was buried in an unmarked grave in the rugged mountains of Afghanistan. This might help explain why the former Assistant Director for the Counterterrorism Division of the FBI, who headed the FBI investigation into the 911 attacks, said in 2002 that he believed that bin Laden was dead. This might help explain why Pakistani President Musharaf said in 2002 that bin Laden is probably dead, after reports surfaced that he had been in the final stages of kidney failure when he received a renal dialysis machine in June 2000. In order for the dialysis machine to function, it needs clean water, a sterile environment and, most importantly, electricity. This might help explain why Mossad, the Israeli intelligence agency, announced in 2002 that bin Laden is "probably dead." This could possibly help explain how President Bush can honestly say: "Look, I don't know where he is . . . okay?" This may shed new light on a statement from "Buzzy" Krongard, the number three man at CIA, when he said, "You can make the argument that we're better off with him (at large)."

Even though our technology can supposedly read license plates from space, his death could explain why he remains unreachable by U.S. Special Forces — why, despite advanced satellite tracking, drone surveillance and ultrasophisticated image detection, we can't locate a severely handicapped super terrorist and part-time political pundit. Instead, we can always find some old or made-up video footage to help perpetuate terror.

9

The busy ATC controllers initially lost AA11 because they would have expected any primary return to show up somewhere along the planned course. ATC reception of AA11 was down to just one more blip on the screen identical with the dozens of small private aircraft in the vicinity that were not required to have a transponder. ATC's natural first reaction was that AA11 was having some sort of electronic malfunction.

This confusion was designed to buy time to complete the mission, which was planned to be over long before any of the four commandeered airliners could be shot down by the military fighters. The tactical planners for the Raiders probably figured that ATC wouldn't be 100 percent sure that AA11 was hijacked until after it had disappeared from the primary radar over Manhattan and they started getting reports that the north tower was on fire. In theory, turning the transponder off would buy the Raiders time — 25 precious minutes — but as it turned out, the Boston ATC controllers were not fooled for long.

10

Within hours of the attacks, the news media reported that this was the work of Osama bin Laden and a frightening "network" of terror. The quick acceptance of this idea was understandable; the raiders were quickly labeled by nearly every senior member of the Bush Administration and every major news media outlet. However, very few analysts bothered to consider the miraculous leap in sophistication from previous al-Qaeda attacks — which had been limited to car and truck bombs, plus the ramming of the USS Cole with a rubber boat in the Port of Yemen. The 911 Commission Report, filtered through the White House's Philip Zelikow and published in 2004, didn't even bother to try to account in any specific or detailed way for the tactical planning, logistical assistance or technical support required for such phenomenal attacks. The widespread assumption of al-Qaeda responsibility dovetailed perfectly with our fears at the time, along with a mysterious and deadly Anthrax scare. Nightmares about our jihadist nemesis were coming true; this was the level of attack we should have expected. Just as important, we needed to brace for further "spectacular" attacks.

An assumption was made that al-Qaeda had now reached the frightening level of capability shown on that day, and America was becoming hysterical. The elderly couple across my street knocked on my door in a panic, after watching Fox News, to say they thought the longtime Mexican neighbors on the block looked like Taliban to them. Airport security was a disaster, unable to distinguish grandmothers or veteran airline captains from suicidal hijackers. I found myself in full uniform, emptying my suitcase in front of passengers and being frisked by a TSA officer. Before I could be allowed to pilot a 767, fully loaded with thousands of gallons of fuel, the straight-faced guard first needed to confiscate my nail clippers. Common sense and dignity had no home as the stress level reached insanity because of the broad new War on Terror. We suddenly found ourselves in an entirely new world: the Post-911 World, cited nearly every hour on commercial television.

Logically, if a terrorist organization could select the perfect airplanes for their mission, slip 19 mostly Arabic-speaking suicidal maniacs and two dozen weapons through airport security, murder four flight crews, and hold hostages at bay while piloting four immensely complicated Boeing 767s and 757s from a high altitude in precise coordination with fellow attackers through crowded federal airspace, navigate for hundreds of miles and deliberately crash into iconic buildings without being shot down by a blanket of military fighters, what could they *not* do?

Instead, what have they done since — or been caught preparing to do — that even comes close? The nation was told with great certainty that the culprit was a shadowy group with seemingly unlimited capability. But since that spectacular attack, al-Qaeda has not been accused of anything more sophisticated than their previously known methods of car and train bombings. Surely, if al-Qaeda was capable of this new reach and complexity, and determined to use it, wouldn't America have seen the execution of at least one or two easier missions? Bombing dams, tunnels and bridges, setting strategic wildfires, even shooting airliners from the sky would be much less daunting and complex than the attacks that actually took place.

11

Communication with American Flight 11 during the climb out and initial cruise, after its takeoff from Logan at 7:59 a.m., was conducted by ATC's Boston Center. Boston Center controllers would monitor the flight's progress as well as all other airliners and private and military aircraft in the vicinity.

ATC controllers are vigilant and precise as they move mankind safely through the skies. The Boston Center controller working American 11 was simply doing his usual outstanding job when the pilots failed to respond to his instructions to climb to a higher altitude at 8:14 A.M. The controller began a series of calls to the aircraft. "American 11, this is Boston Center, how do you read, sir? American 11, Boston." In the next two minutes the controller tried to reach American 11 on the emergency frequency that dominates all others, broadcast into every cockpit within range. He called the American dispatcher in Dallas to reach the plane via American's own dispatch system. The dispatcher tried and also had other American flights attempt to reach them on yet another company channel. There was no answer. At 8:21, AA11's transponder data disappeared from his screen.

As the attack on America began, so, almost immediately, did the response and the defense. The next 15 minutes saw a quickening tempo of urgent communications among ATC, American, the FAA, NORAD and the fighter squadron at Otis. All emergency channels were open. Certainly, the president's National Security Advisor and the Secretary of Defense had access to this loop of communication. The entire military communications system is designed to reach the Commander-in-Chief with lightning speed.

12

Ultimately, the evidence that September 11th was an al-Qaeda operation rests entirely on the confessions of one man, Khalid Sheik Mohammad. We now know that KSM, as he's been dubbed in various reports, learned the hard way to remember his role in 911. Naked and with his feet bound to a wooden board, KSM's lower half was elevated and buckets of water were slowly poured into his nasal passages. Unable to breathe, with water entering his lungs, he would have been sure that he was drowning. The natural human reaction is to survive and the only way to survive is to tell the aggressor whatever he wants to hear. It's that simple. The main reason we don't use waterboarding here in America is that it simply doesn't provide truth, only words to stave off imminent death. After two years of this treatment and a year of sleep deprivation, snarling dogs and humiliation, KSM also "confessed" to every evil act under the sun over the past 15 years — to planning 31 other attacks around the world.

We later learned that his interrogation was videotaped, but the tapes mysteriously vanished. The 911 Commission, taking its cue from the Bush administration, referred to the deranged KSM as a "super terrorist" or "terrorist entrepreneur." In June 2008, KSM appeared in a military court at Guantanamo. Shackled and rambling incoherently, his initial complaint was that the court-appointed artist had botched his profile, specifically that his nose was drawn much too large. After the vanity issue, his next complaint was another ramble about having been tortured for the previous five years.

The President himself informed the nation in a September 2006 speech about the success of the waterboard. Referring to another detainee, Abu Zubaydah, al-Qaeda's so-called planning chief, Mr. Bush said, "We knew that Zubaydah had more information that could save innocent lives, but he stopped talking. As his questioning proceeded, it became clear that he had received training on how to resist interrogation. And so the CIA used an alternative set of procedures. I cannot describe the specific methods used — I think you understand why" — with a pause — "but I can say the procedures were tough. After he recovered, Zubaydah was defiant and evasive. He declared his hatred of America. During questioning, he at first disclosed what he thought was nominal information — and then stopped all cooperation. Well, in fact, the 'nominal' information he gave us turned out to be quite important. For example, Zubaydah disclosed Khalid Sheikh Mohammed — or KSM — was the mastermind behind the 9/11 attacks."

The 911 Commission Report concluded that KSM was the "mastermind" of these attacks, with financial and logistical support from Osama bin Laden. But the Commission's conclusions — or assumptions — are based entirely on thirdhand testimony. Remarkably, no one from the commission was allowed to talk with KSM or even with KSM's interrogators. Americans have been given proofs that amount to little more than words from men behind the curtain. After torturing a prisoner, our government releases his "confessions" to the media with no question as to its authenticity, just as the "confession" tapes of Osama bin Laden give us another unverified source of disinformation. When we consider that only one in seven Americans can find Iraq on a map, the deception is like taking candy from a baby.

Astonishingly, the 911 Commission's final report states the following, within a warning-style box:

> The following chapters on the 911 plot rely heavily on information obtained from captured al-Qaeda members. . . . Assessing the truth of statements by these witnesses . . . is challenging. Our access to them has been limited to the review of intelligence reports based on communications received from the locations where the actual interrogations take place. We submitted questions for use in the interrogations, but had no control over whether, when, or how questions of particular interest would be asked. Nor were we allowed to talk to the interrogators so that we could better judge the credibility of the detainees and clarify ambiguities in the reporting. We were told that our requests might disrupt the sensitive interrogation process.

This testimony wouldn't be allowed in traffic court but in the Post-911 World, this is all we need in order to know who planned the massacre of 3,000 people on 911. The New York City Fire Department lost 343 men; the NYPD lost 23; nearly 200 people jumped to their deaths from the burning towers; United and American lost 33 crew members and 314 passengers; airport security was defeated; the United States military was defeated; the American economy was ruptured; we have warrantless wiretaps, two wars with 4,000 dead American soldiers, another hundred thousand physically and mentally disabled and perhaps another one million dead in the Middle East. Yet thirdhand hearsay from a waterboarded captive is all we care to offer by way of explanation or closure.

Even if we grant these two chapters of hearsay, there is, as noted earlier, still no accounting for the advanced tactical knowledge, logistical support or aviation training required for the mission.

The Commission report purports to describe in great detail the thinking of Osama bin Laden, as told by mastermind KSM. For example, "during the summer of 2001," the report states, "KSM approached bin Laden with the idea of recruiting a Saudi Arabian air force pilot to commandeer a Saudi fighter jet and attack the Israeli city of Eilat. Bin Laden reportedly liked this proposal, but he instructed KSM to concentrate on the 9/11 operation first."

Does anyone else find this idea farfetched? KSM is suggesting a minor hit using one commandeered fighter jet to attack a small Israeli city while he is also orchestrating the logistical nightmare of what would be September 11th. Writing as if they had al-Qaeda bugged and could read the mind of bin Laden, they paint KSM as an absolute genius, multitasking across several continents while pulling off a terrorist assault like no other in history. The conspiracy theory of KSM in the 911 Commission's report is as unlikely as the missile into the Pentagon theory.

13

At 8:19, American 11 flight attendant Betty Ong was on the AT&T Air Phone talking to American Airlines reservations in North Carolina, which was on the phone's speed dial. She reported an emergency — they were being hijacked. By 8:21, just as Mohamed Atta switched AA11's transponder to the off position, the reservations agent passed the call to the on-duty manager in American's operations center in Fort Worth. Ong relayed that the aircraft was under attack, passengers had been stabbed, the cabin was full of mace, she couldn't breathe, and two flight attendants had been stabbed. When American operations placed a call to Boston Center ATC at 8:29 to say that the aircraft had been hijacked, Boston Center was already well aware of this fact. The evidence confirms that there was swift communication along the reliable network of the aviation world — just a few minutes from Atta's full takeover to its recognition.

14

The hijackers' training records from several U.S. flight schools indicate that they were marginal pilots, at best, even in single-engine airplanes. In early 2000, three of the pilot/hijackers are heavily documented at a small flight school near Venice, Florida, while the fourth attended schools in Arizona and California. This would account for the basic flight training of the pilots but in no way can explain the expert level of airmanship required for the 911 hit.

Dozens of reports focused on the pilot/hijackers Mohamed Atta, Hani Hanjour, Ziad Jarrah and Marwan al-Shehhi. Flight instructors around the United States told similar stories of attempting to train them. All four had a very difficult time in their basic training on small, single-engine airplanes. The English-speaking instructors repeatedly cited the language barrier with the Arabic-speaking students as a major obstacle and said that they had encouraged the students to quit. Obviously, this language issue had found a solution by 911; the only logical solution is that Arabic-speaking flight instructors were used, more specifically, Arabic-speaking Boeing flight instructors.

By using small flight schools for basic flight training, the cell remained below the radar, while the pilots' documented use of the schools could be counted on later to provide some sort of explanation (albeit a very weak one) as to how they learned to fly these complicated heavy jets, and might help keep investigators off the trail of the real training. But the leap from a small 4,000-pound single-engine propeller airplane to a 300,000-pound twin-engine jetliner needs a specific explanation. For instance, it took me 20 years, dozens of ground school courses and 15,000 hours between my first lesson and taking command of my first commercial airliner. Adding computer games and outdated simulators to their training was a helpful step, but until they actually felt the yoke and added the hours of experience it takes to understand the momentum of a heavy 767, they would be all over the sky and completely out of control. Not only were they under control, they flew above the average skills required to operate in an airline environment. This miraculous leap has only one explanation: expert and repeated training in the actual Boeing 757 or 767. And by all indications, this took place in the final months of preparation, during the spring and summer of 2001.

There are two different worlds in aviation — the general single-engine airplane world with a service ceiling of 10,000 feet and a top speed of around 200 miles per hour, and the commercial swept-wing jetliner world at 40,000 feet and Mach numbers for speed calculations. Little within that first world prepares the pilot for the second, high-altitude world.

So began my search for Middle Eastern operators of Boeing airliners. Because the hijackers were mostly Saudi Arabian, the firm of Dallah Avco, a Saudi operator of multiple private Boeing airliners, soon stood out as a focal point. To my amazement, I immediately discovered that Congressional investigators had already linked Dallah Avco with the actual hijackers. Omar Bayoumi, a Dallah employee and operative within the Saudi Ministry of Aviation, had provided housing and basic support for three hijackers: Nawaf al-Hazmi, Khalid al-Mihdhar and the pilot/hijacker of American 77, Hani Hanjour.

FBI evidence of the cell would confirm that the hijacking team of American 77 had formed and operated separately with direct financial support from top-level members of the Saudi government, bitter enemies of al Qaeda. The picture was beginning to clear.

From this point in the research, the guilt needle began pointing steadily toward Saudi Arabia, in part because 15 of the 19 hijackers were Saudis. With every new piece of evidence, that needle does not fluctuate. As the focus narrowed on San Diego, the footprints of a large Saudi contingent began to appear. Congressional investigators had found, within buried FBI files, evidence that United States Senators would later call "undeniable" that top Saudi officials had known that terrorists were entering the U.S. beginning in 2000 in preparation for some sort of attack. These same officials are among those who work with American oil companies and regulate the flow of crude oil to the United States, the same Saudi officials that regulate the price that has gone from $30 per barrel to over $140 post 911.

One Saudi official in particular, Prince Bandar bin Sultan, Saudi Ambassador to the United States from 1983 to 2005, was quickly traced to direct funding of the hijackers, through cashier's checks, not from him he would say, but from his wife. Alabama Senator Richard Shelby, Maine Senator Susan Collins and Florida Senator Bob Graham learned that Saudi officials had directed agents in the United States to assist the future hijackers. These senators would quietly back out of the investigation after the White House threatened them with "leaking classified information" and a criminal probe. Senator Graham was told in no uncertain terms to back off and shut up in telephone calls from Vice President Cheney. This evidence alone on the Saudis provided more plausibility than two chapters of KSM's ramblings. Here was opportunity to provide airplanes and instructors for hijackers who were solidly linked to Saudi operatives working for Prince Bandar.

Something about this jogged my memory. In the spring and summer of 2001, I had noticed an odd airplane frequently parked on the corporate ramp at Lindbergh Field in San Diego. My schedule in 2001 was heavy with San Diego trips and I became curious about the highly unusual airplane with its tail number registration HZ-124. The heavy four-engine Airbus A340, normally configured for 400 seats and painted with airline livery, was unmarked and painted like a private jet. A search of the tail number disclosed that the owner was Prince Bandar bin Sultan, Saudi Arabia's Ambassador to the U.S.

The Saudi aviation presence in San Diego was part of the puzzle. Dallah Avco could easily provide the Boeings, simulators, instructors and all the required training needed to explain the hijacker's flying proficiency. The remaining mystery was where the training took place.

As I read through the 911 Commission's report, I noticed that something had drawn all the hijackers out west on several occasions. The 911 Commission reported that each pilot/hijacker had made multiple trips to Las Vegas in the spring and summer of 2001; the commission had "no explanation" for this destination. But, logically, the vast Mojave and Sonoran Deserts would be the perfect training ground for practicing a high-to-low-altitude, coordinated attack.

Initially, I focused on the many airline storage airports scattered throughout the southwestern deserts, where various airliners come and go without drawing much attention. Major airlines operate leased aircraft owned by investment banks. As an airline's fleet requirements change, planes are routinely parked while new lease agreements are negotiated. The dry desert preserves the planes' avionics and interiors while they sit, sometimes for years at a stretch. As I conducted a search throughout the deserts using Google Earth, one airport north of Tucson began to stick out.

At the same time, from several old Iran-Contra sources I began hearing about a hush-hush airport used by the government contractor and mercenary outfit Blackwater, to train covert, special operations flight crews. I soon learned that major flight training had been conducted in the middle of the night with military and civilian airplanes in top-secret fashion. Blackwater is one of several operators that use the very airport I had run across — Pinal Airpark, a secluded desert facility near the town of Marana, Arizona, and near the former home of Saudi Arabian pilot Hani Hanjour, the hijacker pilot of American 77. I discovered that over 80 perfectly airworthy commercial airliners are scattered around the airport and heavily guarded by a mercenary army with covert Saudi ties. The opportunities are perfect to "borrow" a Boeing for unlimited and undocumented air training in the dedicated practice range over the desert. The means and the opportunity to slip hijackers in for training were all in place.

Investigative author Jeremy Scahill had also discovered Pinal and written extensively about it in his 2007 book *Blackwater: The Rise of the World's Most Powerful Mercenary Army*. He traced Pinal's four-decade history of clandestine paramilitary activity, from Vietnam and the famous opium cargo outfit dubbed Air America to today's government contracts in the "War on Terror," such as the so-called Torture Taxi flights to U.S.-run detention facilities in Afghanistan. Scahill reports that these untraceable contracts govern operation of Blackwater's fleet of Casa 212 cargo planes that frequent Pinal. He reports that Blackwater's president Gary Jackson has been bold in bragging that Blackwater's "black" contracts are so secret, he could not tell one federal agency about Blackwater's work with another.

"Air Blackwater," previously known as Aviation Worldwide Services, formed in early 2001, just when the 911 hijackers were in the final stages of training. Public statements said they were to provide "military training operations and aviation transport" for the U.S. government. AWS was then acquired by Blackwater in 2003, as the Iraqi occupation was getting under way. Gary Jackson announced that the new aviation department "complements our strategic goal of providing a 'one stop' solution for all of our customer's security and tactical training needs." "Tactical training," of course, raises a red flag. Evergreen International, an aviation company whose board includes the former head of the CIA's air operations, has taken over management of Pinal while the government doles out no-bid, untraceable "black" contracts to Blackwater, Aero Contractors, International Air Response, Evergreen, SA Incorporated and a host of others.

15

At 8:21, the transponder was turned off and Boston Center lost the data from AA11 but still had the primary radar return blip of the aircraft with each sweep of the quick moving radar. American 11's blip had turned on a direct route to the south, toward Manhattan.

At 8:23, Mohamed Atta made a mistake. The communications panel of the Boeing 767 sits between the captain and the first officer just aft of the throttle quadrant. There are dozens of tiny buttons on this particular panel, some of which select one of the aircraft's five radios to transmit on and others of which select the radio to receive transmissions directed at the aircraft. Frequent passengers may recall hearing the occasional errant radio call over the P.A. that had been intended for ATC. It is a common mistake that is usually made because of a distraction. Occasionally, ATC might hear an announcement intended for the passengers on the P.A. system.

Atta's mistake is understandable, considering the violent takeover of the cockpit. Blood was surely everywhere as he sat at the fresh murder scene, the seat still warm from the captain who was now bleeding to death on the floor behind him. But Atta had been well trained for this mission and he had been trained to make an announcement to the passengers in an attempt to pacify them enough to buy the time required to complete the mission.

In his heightened state, he must have looked down at the dozens of switches and couldn't remember which was which, so he hastily transmitted on the last setting that had been selected by American's pilots. The hijackers had begun the electronic hide and seek with ATC and the military fighter jets that would soon be airborne. In his haste, Atta transmitted to Boston Center when he thought he was transmitting over the P.A. to the passengers. He picked up the mike at 8:23 A.M., "We have some planes. Just stay quiet and you'll be okay. We are returning to the airport."

A few seconds later, "Nobody move. Everything will be okay. If you try to make any moves, you'll endanger yourself and the airplane. Just stay quiet."

What Atta didn't know was that he had just given away the secret and consequently, at 8:23 Boston Center was completely aware that American 11 had been hijacked. Meanwhile, flight attendant Betty Ong was calmly and professionally giving a blow-by-blow account to American Operations in Fort Worth from Flight 11's back cabin.

16

It takes a close reading of an innocuous-looking statement within the 911 Commission's report to realize that a huge entourage of the longtime Saudi Intelligence Minister, Prince Turki al Faisal, was in Las Vegas on September 11, 2001. Tucked in the back of the report was an account of three separate chartered airliners carrying dozens of Saudis, departing from Las Vegas on midnight transatlantic flights beginning on September 19th.

We now know that this group, including Prince Turki, with deep connections to Saudi Arabia's secret police, was in Las Vegas during the time that the 911 Commission could not explain why all the hijackers had made trips to Las Vegas. The roster of Saudi officials in the United States on September 11 includes the Defense Minister, the Minister of Foreign Affairs, the Minister of Aviation and the head of Dallah Avco Group, in addition to Prince Turki and of course Prince Bandar, Saudi ambassador to the U.S. In addition, the head of two of Saudi Arabia's holiest mosques stayed at the same hotel as the all-Saudi hijackers of AA77 — at the Marriott Residence Inn in Herndon, Virginia — on the night of September 10th. In the week after the attack, there were a dozen chartered flights with high-ranking Saudi officials that left from Las Vegas, Newark, Boston and Washington, all cities, by the way, with direct links to the hijackings. By September 24, 2001, they had all returned home.

The British *Observer* reported that the widely feared Prince Turki al Faisal had a long, mutually hostile relationship with Osama bin Laden. Turki, with American connections (he would become Saudi Ambassador to the U.S. after Prince Bandar), was funding bin Laden's mujahedeen against the Soviets in Afghanistan in the 1980s, but the partnership with bin Laden ended soon after. More recently, the entire Saudi royal family had become the prime target of al-Qaeda for their relationship with American oil companies. Of great interest is the *Observer's* reporting that pilot/hijacker Mohamed Atta left Hamburg soon after making contact with Prince Turki's intelligence agents in early

2000. Atta's destination, after a brief stop in Pakistan, was Huffman Aviation, the small school in Florida where he began basic flight training. He was soon joined by Jarrah and al Shehhi. They told people in Venice that they were bodyguards with the Saudi government and needed to learn to fly airplanes.

The prince's entourage entailed a perfect opportunity for the Raiders to get the needed Saudi Boeing flight instructors into the country, and exit after the attacks without anyone interviewing them. The chartered departures from Las Vegas were a four-engine DC-8 for Geneva on September 19, 2001 with 69 passengers, including 46 Saudis; a Boeing 727 for England with 18 Saudis on September 20; and on September 23, a jumbo Lockheed L-1011 for Paris. Only 34 passengers were listed on that plane, which has a capacity of nearly 400. On that flight was Prince Turki.

No one in the government will say just who cleared these flights to leave without interviewing even one of the passengers. Prince Bandar said on Meet the Press in September 2001 that the FBI cleared the flights. The FBI said that they did not clear the flights.

Prince Turki and Prince Bandar have more connections to Arabic-speaking Boeing flight instructors than anyone else in the world. The means and opportunity to slip the hijackers into Pinal Airpark or other facilities for training were theirs. The motive was a world-changing event. The Saudis would benefit greatly not only from the targeting of al-Qaeda but from an American invasion of Iraq, one that they had begged for after the first Gulf War. Dick Cheney would guarantee Prince Bandar that America was going to invade Iraq months before anyone informed the United States Congress.

In November 2001, Prince Turki expressed his public support for the U.S. operation in Afghanistan, referring to al-Qaeda as an "evil cult." By calling out bin Laden for complicity in the attacks, he would be helping to "sic" the world against his greatest enemy, an enemy that has made several assassination attempts against the Saudi royal family. In the winter of 1998, three buried suitcases had been found in Saudi Arabia containing nine antitank Sagger missiles. The Saudis learned that al-Qaeda was intending them for use against the royal family. Former FBI Director Louis Freeh told *The New Yorker*, "From where I sat and from what I knew . . . Al Qaeda was more a threat to Saudi Arabia than to the U.S. and bin Laden's whole focus was on toppling the royal family and getting the U.S. forces out of Saudi Arabia."

17

At 8:23, the Boston ATC controller began the notification process to get the fighters in the air. His supervisor was over him in seconds; the controller briefed the supervisor on what he had just seen and heard. "Pull the tapes," the supervisor commanded, which meant to have a specialist listen again to the recorded transmission from Atta, "and report back to me." In the aviation world, everything is recorded.

Betty Ong is an American hero. At 8:26, she reported from the Air Phone that "the plane was flying erratically." She held the flight manifest with passenger names and read off the seat numbers of the hijackers who had stormed the cockpit. Her fellow flight attendant Amy Sweeney is an American hero. She was on another Air Phone, reporting seat numbers and saying that American 11 was hijacked and there was a bomb in the cockpit. She calmly said that a passenger in Business Class had his throat slashed and two flight attendants had been stabbed, one seriously. She reported that the passengers in the coach section were under the impression that it was just a routine medical emergency in First Class. She knew better, they had been trying to call the pilots on the interphone, but there was no answer.

At 8:28, Boston Center called the FAA Command Center in Herndon, Virginia, to report that American 11 had been hijacked and was heading for New York airspace. By 8:32, the Command Center alerted FAA Headquarters in Washington that American 11 had been hijacked but the FAA already had received the information from Boston and Fort Worth and were already five minutes into a conference call with the New England regional office. Communication is not a problem in the aviation world.

18

To this point, I have limited my account to the events surrounding September 11th and the questions and events that followed. I have said that key doubts about the official account of the attacks emerged for me because of my experience as an airline pilot. That is true.

But equally important is what I have not said: that the ground for those doubts had already been prepared by a unique series of events I experienced as a young pilot, back in the 1980s.

I was involved — for only five months, but very deeply involved — in so-called "black operations," highly illegal activities that take place in a shadow world in which our government gets private contractors to do the dirty deeds most of us assume and hope our government would never do. Except it does. And did. And in this case the fact that it did is a matter of public record.

I was a pilot in a covert operation running arms, cash and, almost certainly, contraband for private contractors working with Col. Oliver North, who in turn was working with the White House, or more specifically, Vice President George H.W. Bush, in the affair now known as Iran Contra. This of course was the scheme to sell arms — illegally — to Iran to give support — illegally — to the Nicaraguan counterrevolutionaries, or the "Contras." A less widely known, even more nefarious branch of this operation turned drugs from Central America into cash, and cash into arms for the Contras.

As I will relate, the three principal "employees" — contractors — for this operation, all of them pilots, were killed under extremely suspicious circumstances just when they were becoming potential liabilities to the management — i.e., to a secret thread within the American government. I was the fourth of those employees, but a subcontractor. Because my work had ended, and because I was so young and only briefly involved, Uncle Sam may not even have known that I existed, or what I witnessed.

When he finds out, he's not going to be happy.

19

At 8:34, Atta again thought he was talking to the passenger but instead broadcast to Boston Center. "Nobody move please. We are going back to the airport. Nobody make any stupid moves." At the same time, Boston Center was making its first contact with the United States military with the sole purpose to launch the F-15s on alert at Otis Air Force base in Falmouth, Massachusetts, on Cape Cod, 154 miles northeast of Manhattan. The jets were called to battle stations after Boston Center made it clear that this was no drill, this was real world.

The call went from Boston Center to the military on-duty Battle Commander for NORAD's Northeast region, Colonel Robert Marr at Rome, New York, who called Otis to order battle stations for the F-15s. Colonel Marr then called General Larry K. Arnold, at NORAD's Continental Region, headquartered at Tyndall Air Force Base in Florida, to get authority to scramble the F-15s. General Arnold gave the go-ahead to scramble and said he'd work on getting the shootdown authorization: He testified to the 911 Commission that he had told Marr, "Go ahead and scramble them, we'll get the authorities later." General Arnold knew he needed one person to begin the protocol, the President of the United States. General Arnold called the White House at 8:36.

After the first airplane hit the north tower, evidence indicates that U.S. military commanders made the correct assessment by quickly labeling hijacked commercial airliners as hostile. Fighter jets at Otis Air Force Base on Cape Cod were scrambled when the military was notified. The pilots and their F-15s were soon airborne.

The use of airliners as weapons may have come as a shock to most Americans, but the scenario had been practiced by the U.S. military on several occasions. And if there is one communication system that is superior to the airline industry's, it is that of the command chain within the United States military that leads directly to the Commander-in-Chief.

20

On a fine Key West night in June 1984, I stood on the tarmac next to my Learjet and watched as a four-engine Vietnam-era cargo plane was loaded with crate after crate of M-16s and ammunition. The work was precise and clean. Six athletic men in black t-shirts and black pants loaded the entire plane in less than ten minutes. After the weaponry came a lawn mower, a dozen weed-whackers, some covered pallets, and finally, among the last items loaded, two shiny new Harleys. All of this had come out of a Ryder truck, and all of it was done in a flash. The loaders jumped back into the truck like a military drill team and the Ryder sped away as its cargo door was pulled down on the fly.

The gates to the tarmac opened as if on cue, just long enough to let the anonymous rental truck out, and in one more blink of an eye there was no sign that anything had ever happened. However, the operation I had just witnessed left a lasting impression. I remember the sick feeling that I was witnessing some sort of major heist. Twenty-some years later, and after a decade of research, I understood that it was indeed a moment from one of the greatest crimes in American history and that I had been used in the scheme.

My unbelievable good fortune in having landed a job far above any normal expectations kept me mute as a potential whistle blower. I had suddenly landed a great position in a tough pilot market and was now cruising at high altitude as the captain of a swift Learjet, jumping around the country as if it were my backyard. It was the sweetest gig I could imagine and I was hardly concerned that there was never a paycheck, just a sack full of twenties every now and then from the jet's owner. On that night in Key West it would have seemed slightly awkward for me to stop everybody to ask what the hell was going on. I acted like a typical new hire — eyes open, mouth shut.

For months, I flew in a bubble of cash and naive tranquility. I knew that landing in the middle of the night in all kinds of remote airports with nary a visit or a word from any form of authority or law enforcement meant that this activity had the green light from higher up. The pattern of flying was complicated and secretive.

I had been hired by Barry Seal, a gregarious man of forty with a quick wit and photographic memory. Barry was becoming a legend around the backwaters of southeast Louisiana. We had all heard the rumors around the aviation world that he was a covert agent of God-only-knew-which government agency. He had accumulated a wide assortment of airplanes and helicopters and would appear out of nowhere at Lakefront or any other Gulf Coast airport and disappear just as quickly, usually in a black Mercedes or black Hughes helicopter.

When Barry Seal found me, I was a contract charter pilot in my early twenties based at Lakefront. Seal had called me just after the Learjet charter company I was flying for had fallen on hard times. He made an offer I could not refuse: Fly his Learjet for a ton of cash. I was catapulted into a wild world of coordinated activity within a cloud of secrecy. Our operation took us all over the country and I was trained to leave no tracks. Everything from jet fuel to hotel suites was paid for out of a seemingly endless supply of Ben Franklins. One afternoon I accompanied Seal to a house in Columbus, Ohio, with an entire bedroom and a closet jammed full of twenties and one hundred dollar bills. I soon found that he had similar houses in New Orleans and Houston. Traveling with Barry was never routine and wherever we went, there were always armed guards, at least three at all times, their gun handles protruding above the belt in the back. They would patrol our driving routes and station themselves around any hotel where we stayed.

We would land in West Palm Beach or Houston or New Smyrna or Phoenix or Lauderdale or L.A. or Tampa or Washington or Columbus or San Jose or the obscure but key town of Mena, Arkansas, and walk to the parking lot of the general aviation terminal to find an ignition key lying on the right rear tire of a beat-up Chevy. Each car looked the same, always a Chevy, always beat up, but always with an engine that ran like something out of NASCAR. In each trunk, without fail, Mr. Seal would find a .44 caliber and a stack of Franklins.

Anywhere we went, Barry would hand me a new digital beeper and I was never certain when it would light up with orders to launch. My orders were always short but very specific, typically something like "west ramp Baton Rouge one-nine-zero-zero" which meant the general aviation ramp at 7 P.M. He expected that I arrive on time and not a minute early and not a minute late. It might be two in the morning or two in the afternoon but I was always to have one engine running and the entry door unlocked. Once Barry was safely inside the plane, he would roar, "Haul ass!" and I would immediately taxi to the runway and get airborne. I had no idea who might be in pursuit as I met a new adventure each day and tried, but usually failed, to anticipate Seal's next move.

Barry called one night in San Francisco to tell me to take off from Runway 28L at two in the morning and meet him on the corporate ramp in Reno. He hung up, as usual, without any further instruction. As an ingenious job incentive, he had hired a barely licensed Colombian female to be my copilot. It was lucky that this Lear 23 model was designed as a single-pilot jet, because most of her talents were unrelated to aviation.

That night in San Francisco, she and I took a cab from downtown to the corporate ramp at SFO and by 1:55 in the wee hours, we were requesting Runway 28L. As we made our way in darkness over the mile-long landfill taxiway that leads to the runway in the San Francisco Bay, Barry Seal stepped out into the glow of our taxi light, waving for me. Along with his *blew you away!* smile he carried a Samsonite suitcase. He jumped in with a laugh and we launched toward Reno — but would soon change destination for Las Vegas. Our crazy pattern had become normal.

On that day of the arms lift, I had flown him down to the last pearl of the Florida Keys, a two-hour jump from Baton Rouge. Seal deplaned from the Lear and soon had installed himself in the captain seat of the Lockheed C-123 Provider, while the radial Pratt & Whitneys idled and the preflight loading choreography ensued. In the previous month, we had made many trips to Rickenbacker Air Force Base in Ohio, where Barry had been trained to fly the plane — covertly trained, under secret orders from unknown powers via the Ohio National Guard.

At Key West, Seal left the cockpit setup to his flight engineer and copilot and came down the extended rear cargo ramp to check his load. I was still watching from my spot near the left wing of the Lear. My face must have registered amazement at the spectacle — Barry laughed, then said something about my tax dollars at work.

"Fly back to Lauderdale and wait there til I beep you." He handed me the digital beeper for south Florida. "If I'm not back in 48 hours, I will have died of lead poison." He laughed and started back up to the cockpit.

"Can I keep the jet?"

"Oh, sure, but you might have to fight Uncle for it."

"Roger that."

"Roger this — " he said, turning to me, "check the bag in the rear seat."

The bag was filled with cash — my advance for the upcoming month.

He glanced at my companion in the copilot's seat. "Be ready at any second."

Soon the Provider was on the taxiway moving toward the runway as I watched from the steps of the Lear. The plane accelerated and lifted off before Barry banked to the right on a southwest heading around Cuba, toward Nicaragua. The position lights and strobes were switched off and blackness swallowed the plane as the engines droned to silence.

Preparation for this trip had included trading for the Provider with a Fairchild Merlin plus a briefcase of Franklins, a transaction I had witnessed on the ramp at Daytona. Then there was the training at Rickenbacker and the outfitting of spy cameras in the cargo hold by a "black ops" technical team in New Smyrna Beach.

I would later learn that the mission was to deliver the arms to the Contras in the Nicaraguan jungle, fly over to Managua to snap pictures of Pablo Escobar loading the plane with cocaine, and return to Homestead with the goods, which disappeared into black ops. After the mission was completed, Seal believed that a guy named John Cathey, maestro of the operation, had leaked his name to the Washington *Times*, which blew his cover to shreds. The CIA dark side had used him and then realized that Seal knew way too much. In due course it would be arranged that Barry Seal would never testify, and never haul ass again.

21

At 8:38 A.M., Betty Ong read off the seat numbers of the hijackers. She reported that they were all Middle Eastern, that one spoke no English and one spoke excellent English. They were in the cockpit, she said, and she didn't know how they got in there.

Remarkably, at 8:39 A.M., UA175, which had yet to be hijacked, crossed paths with AA11 just west of the Connecticut-New York border. Atta was at the controls of AA11 and the UA pilots were informed of the crossing traffic that ATC wasn't sure of his intentions. The United pilots reported seeing the traffic passing below them, without realizing that the plane was on a course for the north tower or they themselves were minutes from their own deaths.

At 8:41, in Fort Worth, American Airlines Operations was well aware that American 11 had been declared a hijacking, that the plane was heading for New York City and that it was descending. There were numerous clear channels of excellent information being delivered. Communication is not a problem in the aviation world.

At 8:44 Amy Sweeney stayed on the air phone to Forth Worth. "Something is wrong . . . . We are in a rapid descent . . . . We are all over the place . . . . We are flying low . . . . I see water . . . . I see buildings . . . . We are flying very, very low . . . . We are flying way too low!" At 8:46, Amy Sweeney's last words: "Oh my GOD, we are way too low."

At 8:46, American 11 slammed into the north tower. America's hell was well under way. The unsuspecting people in the World Trade Center would join Betty Ong, Amy Sweeney, and the rest of the AA11 passengers and crew among the first of the almost 3,000 massacred that morning.

22

One of history's most astonishingly successful partnerships has been that between the winners of the 1958 Houston Country Club Men's Tennis Doubles Championship. Of the partners, one was a 34-year-old Connecticut Yankee and United States Senator's son with a narrow focus on becoming President of the United States. The other was a well-connected third-generation Houston lawyer, only 28, who would go on to master the superpower game. These two would synergize as the world's most powerful political duo. George Herbert Walker Bush and James A. Baker III would evolve into a two-headed political monster.

Twenty-two years later, in the 1980 Presidential campaign, Bush's tennis partner had become his campaign manager. In a major push for their first shot at the American presidency, they were blown out of the water by California governor Ronald Reagan. Nevertheless, they would find a way to take over the reins of the real White House agenda.

As Reagan looked toward the general election against an embattled Jimmy Carter, an insistent voice was emerging from the east coast upper-crust establishment. Major donors began whispering the name of George Bush and alluding to his amazing ties to a vast combine involving Texas oil, the CIA and Wall Street. Against Reagan's original inclinations, Bush, who had lambasted him in the primaries by labeling his vision as "voodoo economics," was chosen as the running mate and the geopolitically balanced ticket won a landslide victory.

Then a smooth play was made on the President-elect that would swap out major parts of the Reagan agenda for the plans of members of the Houston and Kennebunkport country clubs. Ed Meese, Reagan's friend, campaign manager and fellow Californian, was Reagan's first choice to be the Chief of Staff. But in the first critical move, Reagan was told that Bush's campaign manager and attorney James Baker would be a better choice because of his expertise in the fine print department, which would (in theory) save the new White House many headaches.

Reagan bought it and on January 15, 1991, James Baker slipped into the large White House office while Meese was given a smaller office and the manufactured title of Counselor to the President (with Cabinet rank). Baker, the Chief of Staff to the President, and Vice President Bush now held keys to all of America's military and intelligence agencies. The ex-Marine lawyer from America's oil capital and the former head of Central Intelligence now held the reins of the government.

First on the hit list was American labor. The Air Traffic Controllers had overwhelmingly voted for Reagan but were soon dumped and replaced by non-union workers. Of course, years later, those replacement workers were demanding a union but the damage had been done and the tone set. Reagan, former head of the Screen Actors Guild, began to appear confused at his own actions against a union he vowed to support.

Airline labor was next. Another Houstonian, Baker client and campaign contributor, Frank Lorenzo, began buying up airlines on steep leverage with no personal assets invested. Abetted by federal judges, Lorenzo had cooked the books on Houston-based Continental Airlines and led the airline into federal bankruptcy court for one purpose: to terminate the billion-dollar labor agreements with the airline's pilots, flight attendants and mechanics. In the end, Lorenzo's bankruptcy model would be used as a gun to the head of airline employees, who had the option of taking massive pay and benefits cuts or watching their airline get sold off in pieces. It would also form the basis for the script of the Hollywood film *Wall Street*, starring Michael Douglas as the Frank Lorenzo clone Gordon Gekko. "Greed," Gekko preached, "is good" — but for airline employees around the nation, the film was too painful to watch. Lorenzo had ripped up signed agreements and sent airline workers and their families into a nightmare of insecurity.

It was difficult to notice, but the nation's wealth was beginning to drain out of the American middle class as the destruction of unions left no one with sufficient power to oppose the greed. Frank Lorenzo ruined the careers of over 100,000 employees at Texas Air, Continental, New York Air and the late great Eastern, my former beloved airline. The new prototype of airline executive, high on self-compensation and low on customer service, robbed dignity from the American workers and shifted assets into shell corporations. This is about the time we started hearing the term, "golden parachute." As airlines and their employees stalled, spun, crashed and burned, the Gordon Gekkos of the world had already bailed out — in Lorenzo's case, with over $80 million in his parachute. Soon, the great American flag carriers of Pan American and TWA would also go down in flames.

The confounding shift went unnoticed by most American voters. Reagan gave great speeches with positive messages accented with humor and perhaps the best timing of any politician in U.S. history. He represented America well while Bush and Baker slipped into the White House basement to run a covert government with CIA, DEA and black ops assets.

The Reagan and Bush agendas rarely crossed paths, and after a Baker briefing Reagan would appear disoriented. Coincidentally, Bush nearly reached his Oval Office target in March 1981, just three months after the inauguration, when a "crazed" John Hinckley, Junior, shot Reagan. Despite Hinckley's insanity, he had been able to learn that the Secret Service would be slipping Reagan out the back door at the Washington Hilton on Wisconsin Avenue and with perfect timing get close enough to the President of the United States with a loaded pistol to hit his target. One bullet missed Reagan's heart by just one inch.

Coincidentally, the shooter's father was a longtime Bush financial supporter and associate in the oil business. The Associated Press reported that Hinckley's brother and Bush's son Neil had met in Colorado on the very day of the attempt on Reagan's life. Neil Bush was listed by the AP as "working" for Standard Oil while the shooter's brother was the vice president of Vanderbilt Energy, John Hinckley, Senior's oil company, which had been under a DOE investigation for illegally fixing oil prices. (Neil, who had tried but failed to get elected to Congress, would switch professions from oil to banking, where he headed Silverado Savings and Loan during the savings and loan scandal, after Baker had become President George Bush's Secretary of the Treasury. $1.6 billion "disappeared" from Neil's bank while at least $200 billion was "lost" nationwide.)

George Bush had missed becoming the President by an inch, but with Baker running the agenda and providing cover, the basement operations flourished, literally under Reagan's nose, and went unreported for over five years. Later investigations revealed that a vast, illegal but lucrative international arms and drug trafficking market had prospered down below. American defense corporations, huge campaign supporters, soon began taking the profits. The documented defense customers would include key nations in the volatile Middle East — Israel, Iran, Iraq, and perhaps most intriguing, Saudi Arabia.

23

The fighters first appeared on the radar recordings at 8:53 A.M. Unfortunately, American 11 was already in the north tower, spewing black smoke from the ignited jet fuel cascading down to lower Manhattan. Meanwhile, United 175 was in the process of another murderous takeover at 31,000 feet over New Jersey. The Otis F-15s would not reach Manhattan in time. "These guys are smart," said one of the military controllers

At 8:55, there had been a flurry of communications through multiple systems. Calls had been made from Boston to Fort Worth, from Fort Worth to Washington, from American 11 to North Carolina to Fort Worth, from Boston to NORAD in Rome, New York, to Washington to Cape Cod to Washington to Florida and back to Washington. A separate call was made from Washington to Florida; this one came from the White House to the presidential limo, which was in Sarasota.

FAA Headquarters in Washington was aware since 8:34 through multiple channels of communication that American 11, a Boeing 767, had been hijacked. Calls to the National Security Advisor came from several channels, including from General Arnold, who was in desperate need of shootdown authority to stop future hostile attack planes. There can be very little doubt that Condoleezza Rice, the National Security Advisor, was in on the upper, secure loop of constantly updated information.

The United States military had scrambled fighters and the World Trade Center was ablaze. There was little mystery — among dozens in the federal communications loop — as to what had happened: American Airlines Flight 11, a heavy Boeing 767, had been hijacked by Middle Eastern terrorists who had purposely crashed that airplane into the north tower of the World Trade Center.

At 8:50 every network was broadcasting a live shot. Among the millions of viewers was George Walker Bush, watching from the presidential limousine, which was equipped with a direct line to every agency in Washington. Surely the president could see the dense smoke pouring from all sides of the nation's tallest building and a gaping hole that covered three stories of the building. Windows had blown out of all sides of the north tower as billowing black clouds caused by 40 tons of ignited jet fuel rose into the brilliant blue sky.

General Larry K. Arnold was entrusted with scrambling Air Force fighter jets worldwide from the NORAD command center in Florida. He testified later that he immediately began trying to reach the president after he launched the Otis F-15s. He had a direct line to the presidential limousine but somehow never got through, a catastrophic failure in the world of military communications. Luckily, the president's National Security Advisor was in her office at the White House when the general called. Defense Secretary Donald Rumsfeld was already at his office in the Pentagon. Phones were ringing all over Washington.

Meanwhile, two F-15s were shooting south from Otis but would be too late to stop either AA11 or UA175. The Raiders' tactical plan had already delivered a stunning defeat to the United States military. But they were far from done.

American 77 had climbed directly away from the Pentagon target after an on-time departure and takeoff at 8:19 from Dulles Airport. Hani Hanjour would fail to initiate the cockpit attack to match Atta's performance on the first strike of 15 minutes after takeoff. The tactical plan for near-simultaneous hits needed the Boeing 757 turning back east by 8:43 to arrive at the west wall of the Pentagon by 9:11.

At 8:33, AA77 had leveled off at an initial cruise altitude of 29,000, just 105 miles from the Pentagon within the perfect takeover window, and began its cruise at eight miles miles per minute away from the target. We can only speculate what the delay may have been, but Hanjour would let critical minutes expire as the airliner jetted out of the 120-mile radius from Washington and Washington Center handed AA77 off to the next controlled airspace to the east, under the watch of Indianapolis Center, at 8:40.

After a few routine exchanges with Indy Center, the flight was cleared to its flight plan altitude of 35,000 feet and to the next navigation point along its cleared route toward the west coast.

The distance began to click up swiftly — to 140, 160, 200, 230, 250 miles to the west.

According to the NTSB report, the flight appeared normal until a turn off course to the south at 8:55, followed by the transponder being switched off at 8:56 as Indy lost the data from the aircraft. As the airplane began to reverse course, it was a whopping 264 miles from the Pentagon and the north tower was already burning on every news channel. When United 175 hit the south tower at 9:02, Hanjour had only closed to within 240 miles. The Langley and Andrews fighter jets could easily intercept AA77, which was still 35 minutes from Washington. If they did not, it would constitute another catastrophic failure — allowing a virtual missile to head straight for the nation's capital at 500 miles per hour.

At 8:56, "American 77, Indy."

At 8:56:32, "American 77, Indy.

At 8:56:53, "American 77, Indy, radio check, how do you read?"

At 9:00:06, "Indy Center calling American 77, American 77."

At 9:03:56, "American 77, Indy?"

24

The Iran portion of Iran-Contra involved the covert illegal sale of missiles and other arms to the Khomeini-led Iranian government during the Iran-Iraq War. While Reagan and his Secretary of State George Shultz announced Operation Staunch, the administration's international campaign to stop all countries from selling arms to the "terrorist state" of Iran, what were Baker and our vice president doing down in the White House basement? Selling arms to the Iranians!

The Contra portion involved arming terrorists who were bombing farms and villages in Nicaragua. Contras was the romantic term for the counterrevolutionaries of corporate America's friend, the iron-fisted dictator Somoza, who had been successful in keeping labor costs at peasant levels for American enterprises in rubber and fruit, but had been booted out by a new democratic movement led by Daniel Ortega. The United States Congress, after many debates on arming the Contras, decided against any funding at all.

Congress passed two initiatives, the Boland Amendments I and II, specifically prohibiting any U.S. involvement in funding or aiding the Contras. It didn't buy the White House argument that Ortega's Nicaragua was a threat to the United States. In fact, history shows that there was never a threat. The stories generated by Baker and Bush about the Soviets supplying arms to Nicaragua all proved to have been manufactured.

According to Bush's righthand man Oliver North, who would absorb most of the flak once the story broke, the White House basement operation took the profits from the illegal sales of arms to Iran and applied them to the illegal arming of the Contras. These were two separate, impeachable high crimes orchestrated by the same fellows: Vice President George H.W. Bush, Chief of Staff to the President James Baker and Marine Lieutenant Colonel Oliver North. They would all indirectly point to Reagan and send the press on a wild goose chase with questions about how much the president knew.

25

At 8:55 A.M., 32 minutes after Boston Center had started the process of getting fighters on its hijacked 767, the National Security Advisor, Condoleezza Rice, was on the phone with President George Walker Bush, who was in the limo outside an elementary school in Sarasota, Florida. He was far from New York but had seen the live pictures that producers at ABC and CNN had already aired of the major fire burning within the north tower. It took three minutes from impact until the pictures showed up on television screens from New York to Hawaii and only that long for network producers to surmise that this was indeed a major tragedy. The caption on the screen read: Disaster at the World Trade Center.

Surely, the national emergency channels that run straight through the National Security Advisor and the Department of Defense to the Commander-in-Chief could match the TV networks' time of three minutes. Flight attendants Betty Ong and Amy Sweeney had both been successful in being patched, from a moving hijacked airliner, through a customer service agent in North Carolina, to American Airlines operations in Texas within seven minutes of the first sign of trouble. There can be no doubt that a general in the United States Air Force in desperate need of shootdown orders and with a direct line to the limo had the capacity to inform the president within seconds that two F-15s had been scrambled from Otis.

General Arnold's entire shootdown protocol was designed to be accomplished within two minutes. President Bush was expected to conduct an open line call with Defense Secretary Donald Rumsfeld, General Arnold and the battle commander, who would radio the fighter jet pilots. That was the simple and strict protocol. Without the shootdown authority, the sophisticated fighter jets of the U.S. military are as harmless as helium balloons.

As for the Raiders, the tactical planners, undoubtedly they were holding their breath, waiting for results. The next ten minutes needed to produce reports of three more impacts. One down, three to go. Soon the new world, the Post-911 World, would be created. The plan at the moment was for Marwan al-Shehhi on United 175 to be in a screaming dive toward the Statue of Liberty before leveling out and crashing into the south tower. He would not disappoint them. The plan was also to have Ziad Jarrah bearing down on the Capitol dome and the all-Saudi crew diving at the west wall of the Pentagon.

The 911 Commission would later attempt to learn why the entire system of defense had failed, from CIA to FBI to Air Force to the Administration to airline security. It was a total, catastrophic defeat of American security, so, naturally, they asked the National Security Advisor for insight. After much resistance and painful negotiation between the 911 Commission and White House counselor Alberto Gonzales, Rice was finally placed under oath in testimony April 8, 2004. If the matter had been left to Gonzales, Dick Cheney and the president, they would have been happy if everyone had just decided to forget the unAmerican idea of investigating the greatest failure of American defense and intelligence in history. Trust them! The administration would look into it and tell us, through the White House press secretary, exactly what had happened and who was responsible.

Rice knew that Gonzales had outfoxed the commissioners by getting them to agree that she would testify this one and only time. She also knew that the commission had another witness scheduled across town, Bill Clinton, just after lunch. The commissioners later wrote that her tactic was obviously to "run out the clock" until the negotiated time was gone. A simple question would be asked and Dr. Rice would ramble on unrelated topics; and she began her testimony by reading a ten-page, single-spaced statement that merely repeated what had been said many times before.

Well into the stalling, Commissioner Richard Ben-Veniste tried to stop this nonsense during the subject of the no less than 40 pre-attack warnings that had been issued directly to George W. Bush over four months. His specific line of questioning pertained to the August 6, 2001 Presidential Daily Briefing prepared by the CIA. "If you could please answer the question!"

Rice: "Well, first . . . "

Ben-Veniste: "Because I have limited time . . . "

Rice: "I understand, Commissioner, but it's important . . . "

Ben-Veniste: "Did you tell the president?"

Rice: "It's important that I also address . . . it's also important, Commissioner, that I address the other issues that you have raised . . . so I will do it quickly, but if you'll just give me a moment . . ."

Ben-Veniste: "My only question is whether you told the president . . ."

Rice: "I understand, Commissioner, but I will . . . if you will just give me a moment, I will address fully the question that you've asked . . ."

This was followed by a two-minute repeat of old facts. When White House–friendly Republicans began asking questions, she would be allowed to ramble on without resistance.

But later in her testimony, Rice made what she might not have realized was a key admission. She said that she spoke with the president from 8:55 until 9:00, which, most importantly, was before he entered the classroom filled with second graders. Within this conversation, the subject of the burning World Trade Center was discussed. Dr. Rice testified that she informed the president that the major blaze he had seen was the result of a two-engine commercial aircraft and "basically, that's all we know." The Commissioners went on to describe a cat-and-mouse game of unsuccessfully trying to extract the remainder of the truth. But if the National Security Advisor knew it was a twin-engine commercial aircraft, the only way she could have known this was through the FAA. And the evidence is undeniable that the FAA was well aware that it was a hijacked American Airlines Boeing 767 from Boston to Los Angeles. In fact, the FAA had known through at least three separate sources for the previous 33 minutes. It would be preposterous to believe that she didn't know that fighters had been scrambled from Otis or that a major terrorist incident had occurred.

At 8:55 A.M. on September 11, 2001, Dr. Rice undoubtedly reported to the president that America was under an attack that he had been warned about in a dozen separate forms in the strongest possible terms for the past four months. The veteran counterintelligence expert Richard Clarke had been screaming at both Rice and the president that a terror attack was coming, and soon. FBI agents in the field had been screaming about strange activity of Middle Eastern men attending flight schools around the country. The CIA said their intelligence for an upcoming attack was "off the charts" and "blinking red." But with each of these warnings came an inexplicable lethargy from the Executive Branch. Virtually no action was taken to warn the airlines or their pilots. Every time field agents sent vital intelligence up the command chain, including actual names of many of the hijackers, it mysteriously disappeared at the Executive Branch level. The White House was consistent in their actions before the attack in that there was no action. Now that the attack was occurring, the no-action response continued.

After seeing the north tower spewing smoke from all sides and through the gaping hole that extended entirely across the north face of the nation's tallest structure, one might expect the president to take some interest. An open conference line with the National Security Advisor, the FAA and the Defense Department via satellite communication in the presidential limo was readily available and had been installed for exactly this kind of scenario.

All around America, from American 11 to North Carolina to Boston to Dallas to Florida to Colorado to upstate New York to multiple government and defense agencies in Washington, D.C., the hijacking and now the aerial attack was known to be fact. The world's greatest communications system is designed to lead straight to the President of the United States for good reason; he is the only person who can launch the wrath of the United States military.

At 8:59, President George Walker Bush closed his call with Dr. Rice. Instead of the conference call, he opted to walk into a second grade classroom as if the world wasn't on fire; as if people in lower Manhattan weren't leaping to their deaths; as if an American Boeing 767 wasn't burning within a manmade hell inside the World Trade Center. While the NYFD donned oxygen tanks and masks and began climbing those 80 stories of concrete stairs, the president simply ignored the massacre and the towering inferno.

26

In our many hours sitting side by side in the Lear, Barry Seal would school me, in his quick-witted Louisiana drawl, on the new corrupt model of American government. Only Barry Seal could point out the soft-palmed Yalies posing as oil men within the rugged landscapes of the Gulf Coast, from the west Texas oil fields to the Florida swamps, tossing out cash to buy the empty suits of politics. There wasn't a politician who couldn't be bought and there wasn't anything a politician wouldn't do for more power. "Power . . . More power!" he would say sarcastically when describing the mindset of southern governors and elected officials who congregated like seagulls on a beach whenever the Texas Mafia, as he called the group led by Bush and Baker, distributed money. Suddenly, laws were ignored. In fact, the entire operation that Seal was running, with government blessing, arming the Contras with cash proceeds from Pablo Escobar and Panamanian President Noriega, was illegal and downright sinister. But just who was going to stop them?

Working with Seal was a wild ride for a kid in his twenties, flying a Lear within a flotilla of armed operatives as we executed a complex mission above the law with unlimited cash. It left a profound impression as Barry and I developed a friendship based on the insanity of our lives, almost expecting it to end in a bloody tragedy. Between Pablo Escobar and the ruthless Medellin cartel, Central American politicians working second jobs as cocaine smugglers, and Ollie North and the White House boys, the only remaining mystery was which of these players would kill us first. Somehow, that made for great comedy. Watching him work logistical problems associated with smuggling cocaine and selling it for arms and ammunition while training a band of Spanish-speaking non-pilots to become skilled enough to drop crude bombs was only a fraction of what was happening. You can't sell tons of cocaine on a street corner and millions in cash needed to be cleaned. There were places to go and people to meet. We moved around in a meandering pattern with the confidence that no matter what local yokel might come along, he would soon magically go away and stop bothering us, usually scratching his head.

The business of the heavy lifting of arms and contraband shipments was always done in darkness, consistent with the theme of "black" operations. Barry took good care of me, never asking me to do anything but support his mission, using the Lear as a logistical tool and never did I leave the United States. I was on constant call to fetch him when he returned from running arms or whatever to Central America and to move suitcases around without ever touching them. Until I read Terry Reed's book *Compromised*, in the 1990s, I wasn't exactly sure how deep this activity went, but his book was accurate in describing Barry Seal and our activities. It is easily understandable that most Americans would never hear about the massive underground operations that brought immense wealth for the seriously connected. It became obvious to me that dropping a billion dollars into someone's offshore bank account was done on almost a daily basis. Operations such as these provided high lifestyles for generations of the well connected and helped consolidate the new conservative power base.

Something else had also become obvious. This group wouldn't think twice about killing anyone who blocked them. Killing people stood in direct proportion to fear, which stood in direct proportion to the intoxication of pure power. For folks such as these, war would be the ultimate power trip. More power!

27

Although the President of the United States was now sitting in a second grade classroom in Sarasota, he held the key to the missiles beneath the wings of the F-15s that had been scrambled from Otis. A ten-minute video shot from the back of the classroom captures the actions of America's Commander-in-Chief in the nation's most critical moments, just as the Raiders were sweating the outcome of their brilliant tactical planning. While UA175, UA93 and AA77 were attempting to defeat the U.S. military, the Commander-in-Chief strolled nonchalantly into the classroom.

While the towering inferno was taking a thousand lives, George W. Bush prioritized a demonstration that second graders could actually read. To make certain, the second grade teacher had practiced nonstop for a week, the same lesson over and over, so that the president could see, with his own eyes, that seven- and eight-year-old African American students could read and pronounce words. The President had flown in an entourage of the Secretary of Education, the Lieutenant Governor of Florida, Karl Rove, Ari Fleischer and chief of staff Andrew Card to bear witness to this event. They had left Andrews Air Force Base near Washington the day before to jet down to Sarasota on Air Force One, with a fighter escort.

The seven-year-olds would probably have preferred a Wild West show or perhaps a puppet show, but may have been optimistic when the star of this show entered the room with a west Texas drawl, "Goo Moarnin!" Maybe it was going to be a Wild West show after all.

Oblivious to the CNN live shot he had just seen over the caption "Disaster at the World Trade Center," George Walker Bush introduced the tall black man with a suit as the Secretary of Education and another figure within the flashes of pictures as the Lieutenant of something and the teacher sure seemed uptight today as the seven-year-olds sat in their new clothes and at attention, ready to perform. It was very clear that they pronounce everything and a mistake might bring the end of the world.

"Great to meet everybody." Bush forced a smile. "I'm real excited to be here. Good to meet you all." He addressed the students, "I met your principal. . . . Thank you for practicing. . . . Really important."

The president took control and asked the teacher to sit down and begin the demonstration. From the very beginning of this classroom appearance, the president smiles briefly and nods and even laughs aloud a few times, but there are cycles of fleeting, nervous facial expressions with eyes that seem hollow and cold, before he returns to the forced smile and rigid posture. Understandable: He's just seen a terrifying scene of an airliner burning inside the WTC.

28

My first flight with Barry Seal was out of Lakefront Airport, New Orleans, on his personal Learjet 23. Barry told me to file a flight plan for Wichita, Kansas. The Lear jumped up to 37,000 feet and we were cruising normally for about an hour toward Wichita when Barry surprised both me and the ATC controller with a request to descend to 17,000 feet. Once we got clearance, Barry closed the throttles and popped the spoilers. We dove like a broken elevator and then, as we approached 18,000 feet, Barry cancelled our flight plan with ATC and we spiraled down to a few hundred feet above rolling green hills. We were surely below any radar coverage as Barry tracked to a target he had pre-programmed into our GPS. A small uncontrolled airport soon appeared at our twelve o'clock and we landed on a 6,000-foot runway. Once on the ground, we taxied to a large hangar where the door magically opened, Barry shut down the engines, and we glided into the building as the door magically closed behind us.

In ten minutes, we had gone from cruising in the stratosphere on a normal route to Wichita to parked in a secure hangar with two strangers opening the entry door. Hell, I had no idea what airport or even what state we had just landed in . . . and I was in the cockpit!

Barry Seal was a junkie. His addiction was not to heroin, cocaine or alcohol but to adrenaline. He needed to be in life-threatening situations or he'd die of boredom. As we sat there for a second, before the man I would come to know as John Cathey opened the entry door, Barry exposed to me the meaning of his life. It was easy to read what he was thinking: *I just blew you away!*

He slapped me on the back and laughed, "Welcome to Uncle."

Inside this hangar, two Piper Seneca twin-engine props had been stripped to the wing root. New long-range fuel tanks were being prepared for installation. Both planes were painted black and had identical tail numbers. Wooden crates lined the hangar walls and two mechanics in overalls were working on different projects. A middle-aged woman sat in an improvised wood-framed office that had been constructed inside the hangar. A Marlboro dangled on her lips as she talked on the black telephone. I would later understand that this hangar was a national hub for black operations, and its location Mena, Arkansas.

Emile Camp, another pilot from Louisiana, emerged from the office to brief Seal about training that was being conducted for a dozen Nicaraguan pilots. In the following months, we would make several flights to New Smyrna, Florida, where the Provider was fitted for spy cameras and GPS tracking devices. Everywhere we went, Mr. Cathey surfaced as the mastermind for whatever the hell we were doing.

Years later, I saw Mr. Cathey testifying before Congress. I had to rub my eyes. Was this possible? Here was Mr. John Cathey as I had never seen him, wearing a United States Marines uniform and speaking with high-flown patriotism of taking orders directly from the President. I knew he was lying and sure enough, he was ultimately convicted of lying to Congress. His new name was mysterious. Everyone was referring to John Cathey as someone else — as Marine Lieutenant Colonel Oliver North.

29

At 8:37 A.M., United 175, another heavily fueled Boeing 767 had just reached its cruise altitude at 31,000 feet after departing Boston Logan and also flight planned to Los Angeles.

"United 175, Boston."

"United 175, go ahead, sir."

"Roger, do you have traffic, uh, look at your twelve to one o'clock about ten miles southbound, see if you can see an American 767 out there, please."

"Roger, we have him, looks about 29 to 28 thousand."

"Okay, thank you. United 175, turn 30 degrees right, I want to keep you away from this traffic."

"Thirty degrees to the right, United 175 heavy."

"Heavy" is added to all flight numbers of airplanes that weigh over 200,000 pounds. This exchange provided confirmation to the FAA that they were indeed tracking an American Airlines Boeing 767, hijacked and heading straight for Manhattan. Ironically, the United 175 pilots were providing critical intelligence about a situation that would lead to their own murders in just 15 more minutes.

At 8:38, while Betty Ong read off the seat numbers of the American 11 hijackers, United 175 was cruising in the bliss of one of those glorious weather days when visibility allows a view from Central Park to Philadelphia. This was about the time when the flight attendants would be calling to bring up the crew meals. The door would soon be opened and the pilots may have recited typical airline food jokes in good humor. Captain Vic Saracini was probably getting his final view of one of the most striking high-altitude landmarks on Earth, the Twin Towers in lower Manhattan, down to his left. He couldn't know that this very airplane would be inside the south tower in 22 minutes.

At 8:39, "United 175, cleared direct Sparta . . . and contact New York Center on 127.17."

At 8:40, "Good morning New York Center, United 175 heavy at three one oh." Three one oh is 31,000 feet.

At 8:41, in Fort Worth, American Airlines Operations was well aware that American 11 had been declared a hijacking, that the plane was heading for New York City and that it was descending. There were numerous clear channels of excellent information being delivered.

At 8:41, "New York, United 175 heavy."

"One seventy five, go ahead."

"Yeah, we figured to wait to go to you, center . . . we heard a suspicious transmission on our departure out of Boston, sounded like someone keyed the mike and said uhh, everybody stay in your seats."

"Okay, I'll pass that along over here."

What the pilots couldn't know was that, at that moment, Amy Sweeney was giving a play-by-play account as American 11 rocketed into the north tower.

At 8:51:42, New York Center controller saw a change in the transponder code of United 175.

"United 175, recycle your transponder, squawk code one four seven zero."

At 8:51:52, "United 175, New York."

At 8:52:09, "United 175, do you read New York?"

At 8:52:20, "United, United 175, do you read New York?"

At 8:53:52, "United 175, New York?"

At 8:54:33, "United 175, do you read New York?"

30

A year prior to John Cathey's/Oliver North's Congressional testimony, in February 1986, after a three-day trip as a new pilot with Eastern Airlines, I had returned to my rented house in Stamford, Connecticut, and switched on Dan Rather. The lead story was all about my former boss. The night before, Barry Seal, identified now as a government informant and former drug smuggler for the Medellin cartel, had been assassinated in a barrage of .45 caliber bullets from a Mac 10 submachine gun. A "simple" drug murder was a plausible explanation, after Cathey/North had blown Seal's cover and it became clear to more players who Barry was, what he'd done, and what he knew. Now, according to government press releases, Seal had been killed by a Colombian hit squad.

Seal had been working for the government in the first place because of his arrest on charges related to the financing of a smuggling operation. Once the relationship between Barry and the Feds broke down, a federal judge handed down a seemingly innocuous sentence. Barry was ordered to report immediately to a Salvation Army halfway house in Baton Rouge — without his bodyguards. Not surprisingly, it was a death sentence. For Barry, lying dead in a pool of blood on the front seat of his Cadillac in the Salvation Army parking lot, the halfway house was a lot farther than halfway.

The last time I saw Barry Seal had been a year earlier, when we met by chance. I was being dropped off at Miami International Airport, just outside of the Eastern check-in. To my amazement, I spotted Barry pacing outside the terminal. I approached to find him severely rattled. He told me that Emile Camp was missing and presumed dead; the Seneca he was flying was last seen on radar during an approach to Mena. I would later learn that Emile had crashed and died that day.

Barry went on to tell me that the IRS had confiscated his home and Learjet and that he feared for his life. He said that he and I were the only survivors of the cell that had been formed to do the government's dirty work. He led me in a prayer for Emile and gave me a bear hug.

I had come to like Barry Seal, despite all the evils surrounding him. Now, in Connecticut, as I absorbed the news of his death, I began to realize it was up to me to try to deliver the message that Barry had wanted and needed to give us.

During the mission to arm the Contras, Barry had been multi-tasking by delivering goods from Pablo Escobar to his employer, Uncle — the covert operators inside the United States government, i.e., Uncle Sam. Barry Seal helped manage a pipeline from Pablo that had two distinct purposes. The first is obviously money. The second would be the destabilization of inner cities via the availability of cheap crack cocaine, marijuana and heroin. This combination led to immense wealth and the power to manipulate the lives of millions of American citizens, imprisoning more than two million.

When I began my research after Barry's assassination, the first shred of truth I found was *Compromised*, the book written by former CIA operative Terry Reed. Reed had written an amazing and truthful account of Uncle's drug trade. He had intimate knowledge of Barry Seal and all the players from the Vice President to the man who enabled the drug and weapons hub in Mena — the governor of Arkansas, Bill Clinton — two men who would run against each other for President.

Terry Reed was able to follow the money trail from taxpayers into the hands of our new powers, connecting the Clintons and the Bushes to the evildoers. According to Reed, the big financial fish was attorney Jackson Stephens of Little Rock, who directed over three billion dollars from Iran-Contra proceeds into a corporate shell game involving Arkansas state bonds. A red flag began waving when I learned that Mr. Stephens is a huge player in tiny Venice, Florida, the site of three of the four hijackers' basic flight training. Mohamed Atta, Marwan a-Shehhi and Ziad Jarrah had all trickled into the place in June 2000. Later, as we examine another Bush-related heist, estimated in the tens of billions, the BCCI banking scandal, we find Jackson Stephens behind slick banking maneuvers that netted billions of illegal dollars. I have since learned that his wife had been the 1988 campaign director for George Bush in Arkansas, where million-dollar campaign loans vanished into thin air.

Reed also fingered John Cathey/Oliver North, General Poindexter and National Security Adviser McFarlane as conspirators in Iran-Contra and in a prosperous drug trafficking operation. Senate and congressional committees would later corroborate Terry Reed's accounts.

It was Barry Seal who first enlightened me about the fact that the new American mobsters, or the Texas Mafia, were masters of media manipulation. They could funnel enough erroneous information through their channels to give Americans the false impression that the Soviet Union was attempting to attack the U.S. through Nicaragua. This was just a warm-up for what they would do after 9/11, during the Iraq War, in the Swift Boat campaign against John Kerry, and on and on.

It became abundantly clear to me that if Barry Seal had been alive to testify, the neo-mobsters and covert operators doing business from the White House basement could have found new residence in federal prison — a history-changing prospect. He knew about North and Bush running the operation, he knew about Jackson Stephens manipulating the cash proceeds, he knew about the involvement of insiders at the Ohio National Guard.

This operation had become too large with too many chances for exposure. Barry Seal's testimony could mean political disaster for Vice President Bush. In the tight-knit world of covert activities, Seal was a loose cannon. Before witnesses could be called before Congress, Barry Seal would be hunted down, thanks to a strategic tip passed to the Medellin cartel. Ollie North would testify, but Seal would be unable to tell his story, owing to his position six feet below the surface in Baton Rouge. The Bush legacy would go on.

31

The young African American teacher was all business. We can suppose that she felt the entire weight of the world on her shoulders with the President of the United States watching her. A flying spitball wasn't completely out of the realm of possibility and she hadn't slept well over the restless night with thoughts of all that could easily go wrong with these energetic seven-year-olds. The class clown remained in her peripheral vision as her hands trembled.

The whirring of the cameras was only part of this abnormal day of September 11th, 2001. She prayed that the children were going to perform in this heavy environment. "Now read this word from the beginning. . . . Get ready. . . . " She pointed to the poster with a list of words and . . .

"At." The children sang in unison.

"Yes! At." She moved to the next word on the list that was mounted on the easel. "Read this word, the fast way." The emphasis was on 'fast'.

"Ape!" They all responded perfectly, just as practiced. It was going very well.

"Yes, ape."

"Get ready to read all the words on this page without making a mistake. . . . "

The president seemed to find a comfortable spot to focus as he stared down to the floor between the students and the teacher's chair, not smiling and not following along before catching himself and snapping a slight smile. The teacher was in a zone. "Read this word the fast way," she commanded.

"Cat!"

"Yes, cat. . . . Get ready. . . . "

"Can!"

"Yes, can. . . . Get ready. . . . "

The president seemed preoccupied. Fighters had been scrambled but they were as useless as spitballs without shootdown authority. He could be sure of that. The teacher, to his left, barked out another order. "Get ready to read these words the fast way . . . . " She pointed with a pencil to the poster board. "Get ready . . . . "

"Cane!"

"Yes, cane . . . ." Bush seemed to perk up and smiled over the students with a mouth smile.

The teacher: "Boys and girls, you're going to read these words again. . . . "

The president's smile disappeared, briefly looking to the students with a head nod.

"Remember . . . " said the teacher, "what you say when there's an 'e' at the end of the word. . . ." She glanced again over to the president. But he clearly wasn't paying much attention. "Get ready . . . . "

"Can!"

"Yes, can . . . . Get ready . . . . "

The president stared back to the same spot on the floor without a smile. His posture had hardly changed since he took the swivel chair next to the teacher. He nodded his head.

32

After Congress specifically and expressly banned U.S. funds for the Contras, Prince Bandar bin Sultan of Saudi Arabia arranged for cash from the illegal arms sales to be laundered by a Cayman Islands bank, all under the direction of Vice President Bush, who would thereafter lie about his involvement. Bandar would also fund the illegal arming of the Contras, through one of his Swiss bank accounts. Had this financial arrangement been used in an action against the United States, it would undoubtedly, and correctly, have been described as the illegal funding of a terrorist group.

In a letter Ollie North wrote Prince Bandar (as reported by William Simpson in 2006 in *The Prince: The Secret Story of the World's Most Intriguing Royal, Prince Bandar bin Sultan*): "My Friend, Next week, a sum in excess of $20 million will be deposited in the usual account. . . . It should allow us to bridge the gap between now and when the vote is taken and the funds are turned on again." In fact, those funds from Congress would never be turned on again. North said the money should be used to "redeploy and hide Contra forces." These forces would be involved in brutally assaulting Nicaraguan farmers and their families. "This new money will provide great flexibility we have not enjoyed to date" and help "train the forces" (training that Barry Seal was supervising) "and volunteers to develop a regular air resupply operation." North later confirmed that "it was a deal that was never supposed to be exposed to the light of day; nor was the fact that Saudi Arabia was the key financier."

Bandar was quoted as saying, in *The Prince*, that he knew this deal was "politically dicey." North would testify in front of Congress that Bandar "had sought to keep under wraps his role in funneling millions through a Swiss bank account" and "he was promised we were going to keep it a secret, and we tried." When the secret was spilled, the Contra special prosecutor started asking embarrassing questions and Bandar refused to cooperate, claiming diplomatic immunity. The prince simply denied the story and on

October 21, 1986 would issue the following statement from the Saudi Embassy in Washington: "Saudi Arabia is not and has not been involved either directly or indirectly in any military or other support activity of any kind for or in connection with any group or groups concerned with Nicaragua."

George Shultz, the Secretary of State at the time, was a close Reagan ally. This entire Contra episode was enormously aggravating to him as well as to Reagan. He made it clear that he pressed the matter with Chief of Staff Baker along with Vice President Bush. In a meeting of the three, Shultz made certain that Baker knew that any solicitations to the Saudis would constitute an "impeachable offense." Bush argued that the deal could be viewed as some sort of "exchange" if they could come up with something to pacify future prosecutors — if, Bush suggested, "the United States were to promise to give these third parties [Saudis] something in return." Shultz would later say that he was not impressed. Reagan was quoted as saying, after hearing about all this illegal activity, "If such a story gets out, we'll all be hanging by our thumbs in front of the White House."

Believing he had the full support of the White House, Bandar watched the congressional hearings on television and the testimony of then National Security Adviser, Robert McFarlane. Funny things happen when National Security Advisors are placed under oath; they tend to tell the truth. McFarlane testified, "It became pretty obvious to the [Saudi] ambassador, that his country would gain a considerable amount of favor, and frankly, they thought it was the right thing to do; they would provide the support when Congress cut it [funding for the Contras] off." He continued, "In May or June of 1984 [this is when Seal made the flights from Key West] a 'foreign' official [he later identified Bandar] offered to donate . . ."

Strangely, McFarlane, an ex-Marine, had a near-death experience the previous night when he was rushed to the hospital after an apparent drug overdose. Bandar was quoted later, "He is no longer a friend." Fortunately for all of these players, Barry Seal couldn't make it in to testify. His assassination had taken place back in February of this interesting year.

Bandar explained in *The Prince* about the Congressional testimony of his former friend, the National Security Advisor. "He spilled his guts and let me down. The time I lied to the media I said, 'We have nothing to do with it and America never talked to me about it' — because that is what he and I agreed to say. I said to him, 'Look, I don't care what the truth is; if you're going to tell some story, let's tell it together. If it's a lie, then let's lie together. If it's the truth, then let's tell the same story. But you're going to kill yourself or me if we tell different stories.'"

Bandar continued with his outrage at McFarlane, "And he sits in front of the whole world in Congress and says, 'I must confess, Prince Bandar of Saudi Arabia called me one day and said, Come on over — we want to help you and the Contras — can we give you twenty-five million?'" Bandar continued, "He not only lied, because I didn't give a damn about the Contras — I didn't even know where Nicaragua was — but he came to me in the middle of the night saying, 'Look, we need help, ' etc., etc., and I said 'Fine, but has the president authorized this?' McFarlane said, 'I will take you there to see him and he will say Thank you.' I said, 'Fine, that's all I need.' "

The boys in the basement pointed down to North and lesser players. Ollie showed up at Congressional hearings in his Marine dress blues and the bewildered country could only see the uniform and a very patriotic young soldier who was just doing what his president wished. He was later indicted on 16 felony counts and only convicted of three: aiding and abetting in the obstruction of a congressional inquiry, destruction of documents and accepting an illegal gratuity. He was given a three-year prison sentence, which was suspended, a $150,000 fine and 1,200 hours of community service. On July 20, 1990, however, all the convictions were overturned by a federal appeals court and the sentences were vacated.

A congressional report on the scandal stated that the Administration exhibited "secrecy, deception and disdain for the law." Congress noted that President Reagan had been unaware of most, if not all, of the illicit activity, leaving Vice President Bush and the president's Chief of Staff as the highest-ranking covert operators. Large volumes of documents relating to the scandal were destroyed or withheld from investigators by administration officials. With the official White House podium churning out confusing disinformation, Reagan became labeled as the Teflon president while Bush assumed the role of an invisible "wimp" — a covert operator's dream. Nothing could have been farther from the truth.

The U.S. Senate Committee on Foreign Affairs reported in 1988 that members of the State Department "who provided support for the Contras were involved in drug trafficking . . . and elements of the Contras themselves knowingly received financial and material assistance from drug traffickers." The Senate Foreign Relations Committee in 1989 concluded that "senior U.S. policy makers were not immune to the idea that drug money was a perfect solution to the Contras' funding problems."

The congressional report went on to say that "the Contra drug links included . . . payments to drug traffickers by the U.S. State Department of funds authorized by the Congress for humanitarian assistance to the Contras, in some cases after the traffickers had been indicted by federal law enforcement agencies on drug charges, in others while traffickers were under active investigation by these same agencies." Former DEA agents have testified that drug trafficking was conducted with full knowledge of the CIA. The agents further alleged that investigations were hindered by U.S. government agencies.

In 1996, prize-winning investigative journalist Gary Webb wrote a series for the *San Jose Mercury News* that linked the CIA to the distribution of crack cocaine in the 1980s into Los Angeles, the profits having been funneled to the Contras. Webb found that the influx of Nicaraguan-supplied cocaine had fueled the widespread crack epidemic that swept through urban areas. In 1998 CIA inspector general Frederick Hitz confirmed much of what Webb had alleged, reporting that Contra-related entities involved in the drug trade had been protected from law enforcement by the Reagan-Bush administration. The report also showed that Oliver North and the NSC were aware of these activities. A report later that same year by Justice Department Inspector General Michael Bromwich came to similar conclusions.

On December 11, 2004, Gary Webb died from two gunshot wounds to the head, shots described in media reports as self-inflicted, an unprecedented feat.

On January 29, 1997, *The Wall Street Journal* reported on activities at the Mena, Arkansas, airport that involved then-governor Bill Clinton in a cover-up of illegal drug trading activity. The article stated:

"At the center of the web of speculation spun around Mena are a few undisputed facts: One of the most successful drug informants in U.S. history, smuggler Barry Seal, based his air operation at Mena. At the height of his career he was importing as much as a thousand pounds of cocaine per month, and had a personal fortune estimated at more than fifty million dollars. After becoming an informant for the Drug Enforcement Administration, he worked at least once with the CIA, in a Sandinista drug sting. He was gunned down by Colombian hit men in Baton Rouge, La., in 1986. . . ."

In 1992, shortly before leaving office, President George H. W. Bush pardoned six people involved in the scandal: Elliott Abrams, Duane R. Clarridge, Alan Fiers, Clair George, Robert C. McFarlane, and Caspar W. Weinberger.

Elliott Abrams had pleaded guilty to obstructing justice; President George W. Bush appointed him as Special Assistant to the President and Senior Director on the National Security Council for Near East and North African Affairs.

John Poindexter had been convicted of multiple felony counts for conspiracy, obstruction of justice, lying to Congress, defrauding the government and the alteration and destruction of evidence; President George W. Bush named him the new Director of the Information Awareness Office.

John Cathey/Ollie North can be seen on national television as a Fox News icon, having come within a whisker of being elected United States Senator from Virginia in 1994. On election eve Nancy Reagan told a reporter that North had lied repeatedly to her husband about Iran-Contra.

As for the "wimp," George H.W. Bush, on April 26, 1999, a seemingly rather uninteresting event took place in Langley, Virginia, when the Central Intelligence Agency's headquarters were given a new name. Oddly enough, the building was named for a man who had served as CIA director only one year. It was named for a man who had been knee deep in Iran-Contra, BCCI and more, during his term as Vice President of the United States. Yet, apparently it was of great importance to name CIA's headquarters the George Bush Center for Intelligence. This gesture indicates the reality behind the "wimp" facade —a reality of covert connections and unchecked power.

33

The Raiders' tactical plan called for a quick takeover of United 175, another Boeing 767 loaded with fuel to reach Los Angeles. From the FAA radar flight path recording of UA175, the plane went from a normal cruise at 31,000 feet to inside the south tower in less than five minutes. A normal descent from 31,000 to landing requires around 35 minutes of slower descent rates and slower flying speeds. It is extraordinary that from the time Marwan al-Shehhi actually took over the controls at 31,000, he was inside the building in a flash and the Otis F-15s were still 100 miles up the coast, and in any case were still without shootdown authority.

Achieving this second punch to the WTC required flying the airplane at extraordinary descent rates and airspeeds, well above a novice level of airmanship and situational awareness. This high descent rate is an extremely dangerous maneuver, if only because a mere few seconds delay in starting the level-off after the screaming dive would result in a rather large hole in the ground.

All three of the hijacked planes that hit their targets were guided expertly at indicated airspeeds that should raise eyebrows in the aviation community — speeds well above the redline. This threshold is not an artificial number. It is a no-shit, do-not-cross speed for the airplane's structural integrity. Yet these novices were flying at twice the normal operating speed at low altitudes and well above the redline at 370 knots (415 mph) indicated on the airspeed gauge, all the way up to 460 knots (520 mph).

Such speeds make the plane much more difficult to fly and to hit the target — like holding a curve in an eighteen-wheeler at 100 miles an hour. 350 would be smoking — 460 is crazy and would set off some pretty distracting overspeed warnings. It appears that UA175 was in about a 20-degree left bank on impact — at that speed, he did come close to missing the target. For supposedly his first time holding a heavy widebody jet in his hands, this is unbelievable — literally. The screaming descent is even more complicated and dangerous, especially considering the circumstances. It had to have been practiced no less than two dozen times for it all to come down as it did. For example, the first time I actually flew an airliner, a Boeing 727, even after ten years of flying everything from single-engine Pipers to turboprops to Learjets and 50 hours of training in the Eastern Airlines 727 simulator, it was the most intimidating feeling in the world and I was miles behind the plane for many hours to come. I can't imagine trying a high-speed rapid descent on the very first flight, in the very first minute at the controls.

It is a remarkable piece of flying; an expert level of airmanship that kept control throughout the rapid dive, level off and perfect hit on the south tower.

"Mate!"

"Yes, mate! Give yourself a pat . . . ."

The president snapped back to the class, "Yeah!" He clapped his hands and took a search around to the camera filming him from the rear of the classroom. His eyes darted around to the students in the front row. He smiled with mouth only.

The teacher was all business. "Let's read these words on this page without making mistakes. . . . Everybody tell me what this part of these words say. . . . "

For the first time, the president turns his head and pulls back to actually focus on the words next to him. He is now present. The words on the poster were listed top to bottom.

"Rob!" Sang the students.

"Yes, rob . . . . now tell me what the whole word says. Get ready . . . . "

"Robber!"

The president quickly looked away and back down to his comfort place on the floor, nostrils in a full flare while the teacher points to the next word with her left hand. "Everybody tell me what this part of the word says. . . . "

"Run!"

"Yes, run . . . . Now tell me what the whole word says. . . . "

"Running!"

"Yes, running . . . . Get ready to read these words the fast way . . . . " The emphasis was on the word 'fast'. "Get ready . . . . "

"Robber!"

"Yes, robber. . . . Get ready . . . . "

"Running!"

"Yes, running .... Good job!" She pointed lower. "Boys and girls ... read these the fast way .... " Again she emphasized the word 'fast'. "Get ready. ... "

"Smile!"

The president was not smiling as he stared toward the spot, but something prompted him to break out another lip-only smile. "Yes, smile .... Sound it out .... Get ready .... "

"Smiling!" The children held their perfect posture and their perfect responses for the rest of the page while the president sat quietly with an occasional smile, an occasional nod. What else could he do?

34

Prince Bandar bin Sultan would become Bush and Baker's main link into a world of oil kingdoms. This relationship has evolved in the past two decades into hand-holding and immense wealth. The Prince now spends time with the Bushes at their Texas ranch, their Kennebunkport home, at Camp David and of course, the White House. He has had visits to the Pentagon and has been flown on Air Force One.

Bush 41 claims Bandar as one of his closest friends and proclaims that Bandar Bush is truly a Bush family member, although the Saudis are a monarchy, open adversaries to democracy and openly oppressive to women. Barbara Bush even allows him to smoke in her home!

Bandar has held many titles for the Saudi royal family, including Ambassador to the U.S., and has homes in Aspen, Washington, London and Switzerland. He jets the world in his personal four-engine Airbus 340, capable of flying nonstop from anywhere to anywhere. He is a self-described playboy *and* family man! Bush 41 recently celebrated his eightieth birthday on Bandar's A-340 with fellow passenger Jimmy Baker. In *The Prince*, the world's largest arms dealer is described as having been devastated when Bush 41 lost the White House to Bill Clinton in 1992 and busily set to work on an action plan for the next Saudi-friendly president.

Bandar is the son of Prince Sultan Aziz and one of his many concubines. Prince Sultan had fathered 58 children and Bandar had little contact with him growing up. His early credibility revolved around his flying career as a fighter pilot, although it ended with a gear-up landing and a damaged back. In *The Prince*, the flying stories are comical; reading through the obvious bull corn of bravado, it appears that Bandar might have been the worst fighter pilot in aviation history.

The first indication of moving vehicle incompetence was that he wrecked his first automobile while in initial flight training in Great Britain. He "inadvertently" turned off the ignition, which locked the steering wheel just when he needed it for an upcoming curve. The car zoomed through a ditch and landed inverted. His female companion was belted in; Bandar released her seatbelt, which resulted in an injury worse than what she had sustained in the actual crash.

As chronicled in *The Prince*, the fighter pilot was later transferred to the United States for further training and his association with the royal family was soon exploited. Bandar would burn through petrodollars at an unfathomable rate and his Air Force trainers were initially alarmed. His colonel Joe Ramsey was getting agitated phone calls from the local bank about Bandar writing checks beyond the reach of his ten thousand dollar balance. Bandar would make a call to the kingdom and there would be an immediate boost to his account. Soon Colonel Joe Ramsey would become a close personal friend of Prince Bandar.

It wouldn't take long before the older scouts discovered the walking gold mine. Every time that it appeared the prince's days were over, out came a checkbook and doors swung open. He was soon awarded Top Gun for his unit. Of course his unit was not the USAF; it was the RSAF (Royal Saudi Air Force) in which he was awarded Top Gun. By U.S. standards, he would have surely washed out, but he received the honor that led to the miraculous opening of a thousand doors. He was Top Gun! He was a Saudi Arabian Prince! Step this way, our new friend!

Someone had signed Bandar off on the supersonic interceptor F-5, a handful of a fighter jet. He was soon a flying menace. At a 1971 airshow for King Faisal and his guest, King Hussein of Jordan, our Prince was flying the F-5 in the opposite direction of the Diamond formation that would cross over the amphitheater that had been set up for the display. Bandar was to cross beneath the formation but when the formation flew over the tents and the giant sunshade in the desert at Tabuk, Saudi Arabia, Bandar was missing.

In aviation terms, he was a day late but that didn't stop the show like his next maneuver. Because of his tardiness, Bandar had lit the afterburners and proceeded to lose altitude while gaining a ton of airspeed. When he passed over the two kings at an incredible speed, he took down the entire setup in a hurricane of havoc.

Fancy rugs, flowers, chairs, napkins and even the headwear ghoutras were blown off the kings in a vortex of heavy jet fuel and afterburner hell. That was a show stopper.

His father, Prince Sultan, the defense minister, was in the crowd. He walked up to Bandar and finally had a nice one-on-one chat with his boy: "You're court-martialed."

The American working the control tower was quoted as saying, "Sweet Jesus — that was spectacular!"

It was not long before our Prince was making great headway in American politics. With his reputation as a Top Gun fighter pilot, he was led into the arms race as the Saudi expert in aviation matters. His first major arms deal involved the Airborne Warning and Control System or AWACS deal from the United States (defense contractors) to the Saudi government. Bush and Baker led Bandar to Boeing and other contractors. Fear was induced of a theoretical Soviet attack on the oilfields and more theoretical fear of the Israelis and their American-made fighters.

In all, six Boeing 707s were modified with radar tracking equipment and the planes would fly a perpetual racetrack pattern over the kingdom while a 1980 computer system communicated with the ground equipment. This would give Saudi Arabia perhaps five minutes of warning in the event of an aerial attack. AWACS was an arms salesman's dream, a toothless tiger, a security guard armed with mace.

In 1981 dollars, considering that a commercial Boeing 707 sold for around $25 million, six would be around $1.5 billion. To be fair, the extra-large radar antennas on the top of the fuselages would double the price to $3 billion. Let's not forget the computer system at, let's say, an even billion, for a total deal of $4 billion. But with Top Gun in the mix, the deal was announced at $85 billion! — the extra $81 billion no doubt going largely to the aircraft brokers in the Texas Mafia, so that it wasn't long before the Vice President proclaimed that Bandar was now an official member of the Bush family. His new name in Kennebunkport was Bandar Bush. An extra place would be set at Thanksgiving and Bar would make an exception to the no smoking rule as the new Bush fired up Cubans in the living room. The Bushes loved Bandar with all their hearts. It is a love story like no other.

The $81 billion in 1981 would have been enough to buy 3,240 Boeing 707s — a fleet greater than today's United, American, Delta, Continental, US Air, Jet Blue and Southwest combined. Saudi Arabia had bought six planes and a new family from Connecticut/Texas. The price wasn't cheap, but Bandar's new family would have to hold his hand in public.

Then Iran-Contra proved to be another opportunity for Bandar and the Saudi kingdom to swing open more doors. As Reagan made speeches, Bush and Ollie's gang sent arms to terrorists with funds from Bandar, washed and dried in the Caymans so that the pesky United States Congress couldn't see. Bandar would also be the middleman in arms shipments to what Reagan had labeled the "terrorist state" of Iran. It would take three pages to list each impeachable act, but when the twisted facts came out, no one could piece it together. Not only did the criminals go free, one was elected President of the United States.

35

At 9:04 A.M., Chief of Staff Andrew Card approached the president from stage right and whispered into the Commander-in-Chief's ear. "A second plane has hit the World Trade Center. America is under attack." Until this point, a very weak argument could have been made about not jumping into action to get the Commander-in-Chief up to speed on the hundreds of communications that were flying around the military command in the heat of the battle. We now know that General Arnold had been told that the president was busy at the moment, *occupado*, he'll get back to you after the second graders' story is finished.

America has been led to believe that George Walker Bush is slow and borderline stupid. Maybe he is, maybe he isn't. His former classmates at his private prep school, where the president was one of the school's cheerleaders, can hardly believe that he now has an office at all, much less the Oval one. After two decades of cocaine and alcohol use, perhaps he was clueless about the raging fire and massacre until Andy Card whispered into his ear. He led us to believe that he saw the fire from American 11 in his limousine and thought it was some "terrible pilot" — that all that smoke pouring from the gaping hole and all sides of the upper floors was not a big deal. He led us to believe that he had not imagined an attack using commercial airliners. Maybe he didn't remember all the briefings throughout the spring and summer of 2001 and it really was all a big surprise!

But at this moment, the Commander-in-Chief of all American Armed Forces was, without any doubt, told that the nation of 300 million was under a vicious air attack.

The Raiders were surely on edge. This was a bold and risky attack, perhaps the greatest in world history. Surely all within the esoteric circle watched, and waited, as the moment of truth had finally arrived. Hearts were about to explode. Three more planes were out there. How was it going? Those damn intangibles were impossible to predict as they watched the second 767 appear on live television. There's number two! Two down and where are three and four? Hopefully on the screen within the next 60 seconds!

Trillions of dollars have been spent building the United States military defense. As every military commander knows, from the Marine Sergeant to the Army Colonel, to a thousand Naval Commanding Officers on constant alert around the world, to the NORAD Command Center, a quick response is the heart of American defense, and no lethal force can be initiated without action from the President. America was in dire need of a strong and capable Commander-in-Chief to launch a wave of fighter jets and make damn sure that those fighters had shootdown authority.

George Walker Bush had life-saving decisions in front of him. His reaction followed a pattern consistent with his reaction to the dozen warnings of an imminent attack over the previous months. Instead of passing the "off the charts" warnings about an impending attack using airliners to the Transportation Secretary or the FAA chief or to airline pilots, he did nothing. When he was slipped into the Texas Air National Guard in 1971 and was trained with taxpayer funds to fly a fighter jet in combat, he went missing and thumbed his nose at the system. Unbelievably, this man became Commander-in-Chief of America's armed forces. But now was his chance to shine. Would he go absent again?

As Andy Card whispered, President Bush's reaction is consistent with a commander receiving an update on the attack and not an initial attack report. There is no denying that after Card whispered to him, the president knew that a massacre was in progress; that two airliners had penetrated all of our defenses. His reaction was consistent with the wishes of the Raiders — that those fighter jets would not become a problem for the air raid that had begun to slip behind schedule.

America is under attack. No one knows if the attack is going to turn nuclear. No one knows who the enemy is. No one knows if this is the first wave, the second wave or if the attack is isolated or nationwide or worldwide. From the pictures that President Bush saw before entering the classroom, surely thousands of people had already perished in the first towering inferno. Now there was a second inferno. Millions of Americans were on Manhattan at nine in the morning on a Tuesday, thousands within the Trade Center itself.

George Walker Bush's face paled and flushed. He nodded and his posture stiffened again as he darted his eyes toward Karl Rove standing against the wall. The Commander-in-Chief remained seated next to the second grade teacher who had taken one of the two identical copies of a book from the table between her and her visitor. She opened her book and gave a quizzical look to the stiff man who was clearly not keeping the second grade pace. She waited for him to pick up his copy but the silence was too uncomfortable.

"Thank you," she said, while glancing at the world's most powerful man in his most critical hour, when the new world was being created. "Let's take a look at the title of this story. . . . " Again she glanced at George Walker and he finally snapped to attention and reached for his copy on the table.

"Get ready. . . . "

Bush fumbled to open the book.

36

Time magazine ran a cover story on June 29, 1991 that was so sensational and so profoundly disturbing that no one seemed able to put their arms around it or quite accept it. It was too bad to be true. Perhaps the mindset was, if we ignored it, it would simply go away. It couldn't be as bad as all that. Could it?

To get a glimpse of the worldwide roots of black operations and their ties to the administrations of Bush 41 and Bush 43, to Saudi Arabia and international terrorism it is helpful to look at the case of the Bank of Credit & Commerce International. BCCI had the basement boys' fingerprints — Baker and George H.W. Bush — all over it, signifying more illicit, mega-wealth enterprising at the expense of American taxpayers. Judging from the mild reaction to *Time's* revelations, Americans could not believe that there was a new criminal thread within the upper floors of the U.S. government actually cooperating with crooks, terrorists, political con artists and foreign dictators.

Time magazine caught a whiff of this activity, after eight years of Bush and Baker in the White House basement and three more years in the Oval Office. If we plug 2008 research into Time's 1991 article, we get an even clearer picture of the kind of criminal activity that Barry Seal had been telling me about in 1984, of what goes on in the "Texas Mafia" world with heavy Saudi influence.

Time's cover story of June 29, 1991, was titled: "The Dirtiest Bank of All." Following are excerpts. The entire article is available at *Time's* website.

> "I could tell you what you want to know, but I must worry about my wife and family — they could be killed." – a former top B.C.C.I. officer
>
> "We better not talk about this over the phone. We've found some bugs in offices that haven't been put there by law enforcement." – a Manhattan investigator probing B.C.C.I.
>
> Nothing in the history of modern financial scandals rivals the unfolding saga of the Bank of Credit & Commerce International, the $20 billion rogue empire that regulators in 62

countries shut down early this month in a stunning global sweep. Never has a single scandal involved so much money, so many nations or so many prominent people.

Superlatives are quickly exhausted: it is the largest corporate criminal enterprise ever, the biggest Ponzi scheme, the most pervasive money-laundering operation and financial supermarket ever created for the likes of Manuel Noriega, Ferdinand Marcos, Saddam Hussein and the Colombian drug barons. B.C.C.I. even accomplished a Stealth-like invasion of the U.S. banking industry by secretly buying First American Bankshares, a Washington-based holding company, whose chairman is a former U.S. Defense Secretary.

But B.C.C.I. is more than just a criminal bank. TIME has pieced together a portrait of a clandestine division of the bank called the "black network," which functions as a global intelligence operation and a Mafia-like enforcement squad. . . . [which] has used sophisticated spy equipment and techniques, along with bribery, extortion, kidnapping and even, by some accounts, murder. The black network — so named by its own members — stops at almost nothing to further the bank's aims the world over.

The more conventional departments of B.C.C.I. handled such services as laundering money for the drug trade and helping dictators loot their national treasuries. The black network, which is still functioning, operates a lucrative arms-trade business and transports drugs and gold. According to investigators and participants in those operations, it often works with Western and Middle Eastern intelligence agencies. The strange and still murky ties between B.C.C.I. and the intelligence agencies of several countries are so pervasive that even the White House has become entangled. As TIME reported earlier this month, the National Security Council used B.C.C.I. to funnel money for the Iran-Contra deals, and the CIA maintained accounts in B.C.C.I. for covert operations. Moreover, investigators have told TIME that the Defense Intelligence Agency has maintained a slush-fund account with B.C.C.I., apparently to pay for clandestine activities.

But the CIA may have used B.C.C.I. as more than an undercover banker: U.S. agents collaborated with the black network in several operations, according to a B.C.C.I. black-network "officer" who is now a secret U.S. government witness. Sources have told investigators that B.C.C.I. worked closely with Israel's spy agencies and other Western intelligence groups as well, especially in arms deals. The bank also maintained cozy relationships with international terrorists, say investigators ....

The bank's intelligence connections and alleged bribery of public officials around the world point to an explanation for the most persistent mystery in the B.C.C.I. scandal: why banking and law-enforcement authorities allowed the bank to spin out of control for so long.

In the U.S. investigators now say openly that the Justice Department has not only reined in its own probe of the bank but is also part of a concerted campaign to derail any full investigation. Says Robert Morgenthau, the Manhattan district attorney, who first launched his investigations into B.C.C.I. two years ago: "We have had no cooperation from the Justice Department since we first asked for records in March 1990. In fact they are impeding our investigation, and Justice Department representatives are asking witnesses not to cooperate with us."

(2008 note – The chief of the Justice Department's criminal division under former President Bush was Robert Mueller. Because the major players came out of the scandal with slaps on the wrists, many critics accused Mueller of botching the investigation. Mueller was later appointed by President George W. Bush as the Director of the FBI. His appointment came on September 4, 2001, one week before 911. Florida Senator Bob Graham spoke in 2002 of an attempt to bury evidence about the Saudi support for the hijackers, saying that "the administration had found an eager accomplice in the FBI" and that Mueller had become a "facilitator of the ineptitude of the bureau," directly involved in hiding the truth of the existence of Saudi hijackers and their supporters in San Diego.)

> ... Agha Hasan Abedi, the bank's founder and leader until his ouster last year, is a Pakistani. . . .

(2008 note – James Bath, a BCCI director, and Agha Hasan Abedi have been linked in numerous Saudi-Texas business deals in Houston. Mr. Bath was one of two pilots dismissed from the Texas Air National Guard in 1972 — the other was George Walker Bush.)

"If B.C.C.I. is such an embarrassment to the U.S. that forthright investigations are not being pursued, it has a lot to do with the blind eye the U.S. turned to the heroin trafficking in Pakistan," says a U.S. intelligence officer.

The black network was a natural outgrowth of B.C.C.I.'s dubious and criminal associations. The bank was in a unique position to operate an intelligence-gathering unit because it dealt with such figures as Noriega, Saddam, Marcos, Peruvian President Alan Garcia, Daniel Ortega, *contra leader Adolfo Calero* and arms dealers like Adnan Khashoggi. Its original purpose was to pay bribes, intimidate authorities and quash investigations. But according to a former operative, sometime in the early 1980s the black network began running its own drugs, weapons and currency deals.

... A typical operation took place in April 1989, when a container ship from Colombia docked during the night at Karachi, Pakistan. Black-unit operatives met the ship after paying $100,000 in bribes to Pakistani customs officials. The band unloaded large wooden crates from several containers. "They were so heavy we had to use a crane rather than a forklift," says a participant. The crates were trucked to a "secure airport" and *loaded aboard an unmarked 707 jet*, where an American, believed by the black-unit members to be a CIA agent, supervised the frantic activity.

The plane then departed for Czechoslovakia, taking the place of a scheduled Pakistan International Airlines commercial flight that was aborted at the last minute by prearrangement. *The 707's radar transponder was altered* to beep out the code of a commercial airliner, which enabled the plane to overfly several countries without arousing suspicion. "From Czechoslovakia the 707 flew to the U.S.," said the informant, insisting that none of the black-unit workers had any knowledge of what was in the heavy wooden crates. "It could have been gold. It could have been drugs. It could have been guns. We dealt in those commodities. . . ."

....

U.S. intelligence agencies were well aware of such activities. "B.C.C.I. played an indispensable role in facilitating deals between Israel and some Middle Eastern countries," says a former State Department official. "And when you look at the Saudi support of the Contras, ask yourself who the middleman was:

there was no government-to-government connection between the Saudis and Nicaragua."

(2008 note – Thanks to Bandar's confession and bravado, we now know that he was the middleman.)

When you couldn't use direct government transfers or national banks, B.C.C.I. was there to hot-wire the connections between Saudi Arabia, China and Israel." The bank also helped transfer North Korean Scud-B missiles to Syria, a B.C.C.I. source told TIME.

. . . . Sources say B.C.C.I. officials, known as protocol officers, were responsible for providing a smorgasbord of services for customers and national officials: paying bribes to politicians, supplying "young beauties from Lahore," moving drugs and expediting insider business deals.

. . . . The black network was the bank's deepest secret, but rumors of its activities filtered through the bank's managerial level with chilling effectiveness. Senior bankers voice fears that they will be financially ruined or physically maimed — even killed — if they are found talking about B.C.C.I.'s activities. . . .

Businessmen who pursued shady deals with B.C.C.I. are just as frightened. "Look," says an arms dealer, "these people work hand in hand with the drug cartels; they can have anybody killed . . . ." Currently the black units have focused their scrutiny and intimidation on investigators. "Our own people have been staked out or followed, and we suspect tapped telephones," says a New York law-enforcement officer.

The black unit's mission eventually became the pursuit of power and influence for its own sake, but its primary purpose was to foster a global looting operation that bilked depositors of billions of dollars. Price Waterhouse, the accounting firm whose audit triggered the worldwide seizure of B.C.C.I. assets earlier this month, says the disarray is so extreme that the firm cannot even put together a coherent financial statement. But investigators believe $10 billion or more is missing, fully half of B.C.C.I.'s worldwide assets.

. . . . The bank's *extensive use of unregulated Cayman Islands accounts* enabled it to hide almost anything.

. . . . in the . . . mid-1980s, B.C.C.I. became a magnet for drug money, capital-flight money, tax-evading money and money from corrupt government officials. B.C.C.I. quickly gained a reputation as a bank that could move money anywhere and hide it without a trace. It was the bank that knew how to get around foreign-exchange rules and falsify letters of credit in support of smuggling.

— In Iraq, B.C.C.I. became one of the principal conduits for money that *Saddam Hussein skimmed from national oil revenues during the 1980s.* . . . . B.C.C.I. helped the dictator move and hide money all over the world.

. . . .

. . . . Billions of dollars were vanishing. At the highest levels, *B.C.C.I. officials whisked deposits into secret accounts in the Cayman Islands.*

These accounts constituted a hidden bank within B.C.C.I., known only to founder Abedi and a few others. From those accounts, B.C.C.I. would lend massive amounts to curry favor with governments . . . or to buy secret control of companies.

U.S. regulators discovered recently that such loans had enabled B.C.C.I. to buy clandestine control in three American banks: *First American Bankshares* in Washington, National Bank of Georgia *(later purchased by First American)* and Independence Bank of Encino, Calif.

(2008 note – The First American takeover was assisted by Jackson Stephens, head of a powerful Little Rock investment firm and husband of the Bush for President 1988 campaign manager in Arkansas. Mr. Stephens has been the rainmaker in many of the Bushes' political and financial enterprises. In 1991, he donated $100,000 to a Bush 41 campaign fundraising dinner and when George W. Bush was awarded the Florida election in 2000, Jack Stephens made another substantial contribution. The former president told Stephens, "Jack, we love you and we are very, very grateful for what you have done." This remark coincided with a $25 million investment from the Union des Banques Suisses, the Swiss Bank that held the minority interest in the Geneva-based subsidiary of BCCI. Both Stephens and a Saudi real estate investor signed the financial transaction, which was never to be repaid. Coincidentally, Jack Stephens owned a major office complex within walking distance of the Venice, Florida, airport where Mohamed Atta, Marwan al Shehhi and Ziad Jarrah trained for the 911 mission. Witnesses from a local diner reported overhearing a

conversation in which the hijackers were arguing about $200,000 payments to "the families," an anecdote that matches a report in the British Observer of a financial agreement with the Saudi intelligence chief.)

. . . [a] "nominee" shareholder arrangement meant that B.C.C.I. itself remained invisible to U.S. banking regulators. Following its discovery earlier this year that B.C.C.I. owned both First American and Independence Bank, the Federal Reserve ordered it to sell them off.

. . . . In the U.S. millions of dollars flowed through B.C.C.I.'s Washington office, allegedly destined to pay off U.S. officials.

. . . . [Senate investigator] Blum: "There's no question in my mind that it's a calculated effort inside the Federal Government to limit the investigation. The only issue is whether it's a result of high-level corruption or if it's designed to hide illegal government activities."

The Justice Department denies any reluctance to investigate . . . . Yet the evidence of a cover-up is mounting:

— In one of the most mysterious events in the case, B.C.C.I. bank records from Panama City relating to Noriega "disappeared" in transit to Washington while under guard by the Drug Enforcement Administration. After an internal investigation, the DEA said it had no idea what had happened to the documents.

— Lloyd's of London, which is enmeshed in a racketeering lawsuit against B.C.C.I., has fruitlessly made offers to provide evidence of bribery and kickbacks and has made "repeated pleas" to U.S. Attorneys in Miami and New Orleans to seize B.C.C.I. records. Lloyd's accuses B.C.C.I. of taking part in smuggling operations and falsifying shipping documents. The insurance underwriters offered the results of their voluminous research into the bank's illegal activities. The Justice Department attorneys ignored the offers, Lloyd's says.

— The U.S. Attorney General has assigned only a handful of FBI agents to its Washington grand jury investigation of B.C.C.I.'s relationship to First American Bankshares. The department's main probe of B.C.C.I. itself is being handled by a sole Assistant U.S. Attorney in Tampa, who has recently been assigned another major case. Similar understaffing is evident in a Miami grand jury probe of the relationship between B.C.C.I. and the CenTrust savings and loan, whose failure is estimated to cost taxpayers $2 billion. This may help account for the fact that a 16-month investigation has yielded no indictments.

. . . . Experts raise questions about B.C.C.I.'s links to Western intelligence agencies. ...

Still to be probed, with potentially explosive results, is B.C.C.I.'s Washington office. Sources have told TIME that one of B.C.C.I.'s Washington representatives distributed millions of dollars in payoffs to U.S. officials during the past decade.

(2008 note – That particular decade began when Mr. Baker and Mr. Bush moved from Houston to Washington — a decade that started with the attempted assassination of Reagan and continued with AWACS, BCCI, Iran-Contra, the Savings & Loan scandal and the first Iraq War.)

From Time's follow-up article of September 2, 1991:

The Price Waterhouse audit that led to B.C.C.I.'s seizure last July covered only its banking activities. It said nothing about immensely profitable deals in other businesses, notably weaponry. Nor could it account for profits it could not see. And while the enterprise's known banking services are shut down around the world, virtually the full cadre of B.C.C.I.'s black network, arms traders and global operatives remain unindicted, unaccused and at large. The best guess of many of the sources TIME interviewed is that they will simply move on. . . .

37

It was hard to hear the students over the constant camera snaps but they had indeed learned to read. "My pet goat . . . ," the students sang in perfect unison.

"Get ready to read the title the fast way. . . . " The emphasis was on 'fast'.

"My pet goat." The teacher had taken a pencil and tapped in a rhythm between words, making the sound of my . . . *tap* . . . pet . . . *tap* . . . goat.

"Yes! My Pet Goat. . . . Get ready. . . . fingers under the first word of the story. . . . " Bush appeared to be drifting in and out of deep thought and his eyes were darker and he was clearly uncomfortable. But he stared at the pages while the towers burned and NYFD was humping up the endless concrete steps with 50 pounds of equipment and more Raider jets were coming. Only the Raiders knew it was not over. Only one man could stop them. One man held the keys to the missiles under the wings of those fighter jets, the only way to limit the massacre. "Get ready to read the story the fast way . . . ."

"The girl had a pet goat . . . "

"Go on . . . "

"She liked to . . . " As the reading went on, the cameras whirred with constant shooting, "her pet goat . . . "

"Go on. . . . " commanded the teacher. The president had his book open but cut his eyes around the room. "Ready. . . . "

"She played with her pet goat in her yard. . . . "

"Go on. . . . "

America's situation in this hour is grave. After spending endless taxes for a quick-response military with billion-dollar B-2 bomber jets and Aegis class missile ships and four-star generals, all designed to keep America safe, so that our defense is airtight and no one would dare attempt to penetrate U.S. airspace and hijack our airliners, the Commander-in-Chief, for whatever reason, while half-billion-dollar fighter jets wait only for his direction, sits and stares at the floor.

"But the goat did something that made . . . " Something was seriously wrong. Half the class seemed to lose focus, the last part of the sentence was all smeared with indecision. The teacher jumped into action.

"Let's clean that up!" She would tap harder between words while Bush bobbed his head to the rhythm of her pencil.

"But *tap* the *tap* goat *tap* did *tap* something *tap* that *tap* made *tap* the *tap* girl *tap* mad . . . " Bush smiled with the beat.

Millions of Americans and millions around the world were terrorized, completely aware that New York was under a vicious attack with commercial airliners. This was clearly an act of terrorism and it might still be a long way from over. More reports began to surface about missing jetliners. The F-15s were shooting toward Manhattan, and they still had no authority to do anything but watch.

On American 77, Hanjour was late, a full 26 minutes behind the plan. One might assume, as the towers burned on televisions across the country and as passengers on AA77 made frantic calls to relatives, that the Commander-in-Chief would be issuing weapons-free authority to every available fighter jet on the east coast. The Defense Department might be considering firing a missile at any known hostile craft. Who's going to make these very tough decisions? Surely, by 9:20, this hostile aircraft headed for the capital of the United States had no chance to penetrate much further without at least one fighter jet on his wing.

Finally, the story of the pet goat had finished; perhaps now we could find time to start communicating with the events around New York. But first, the Commander-in-Chief apparently felt the need to extend his time in the class and to make conversation.

"Whew! That was great reading!" He remained seated and smiled to the children. "Very impressive." He continued to scan the room. "Thank you all so much for showing me your reading skills. . . . You practiced this, right?"

"Oh yes," said the teacher.

He remained seated. "Reading more than they watch TV?"

"That's right; they read more than they watch TV."

"Oh, that's good . . . " He closed his copy of the book. "Thank you for having me . . . Very impressive . . . " While the president remained seated, the video ended. Tick, tick, tick.

The raiders were certainly getting nervous; 9:11 on 911 had come and gone. Two planes were not on plan. This was not good. What in the hell happened to 93? He had pushed off the gate right on schedule but where the hell was he and where the hell was 77? As we will see, they may have not been in the dark. But for now, let's stick with solid evidence.

Two airplanes were still missing and unaccounted for, yet no shootdown authority had been ordered and no more military fighters had been scrambled, even with that knowledge.

After disappearing within another classroom with Karl Rove, Ari Fleischer and his traveling staff for around 15 minutes, while American 77 descended toward the Pentagon, the President emerged to deliver a written statement at a podium that was set in front of the children. It was the inaugural speech of the Post-911 World:

"Ladies and gentlemen. This is a difficult moment for America." The children stood behind the president and a few were smiling, unaware of what was going down. "I'm, unfortunately, will be going back to Washington after I deliver my remarks . . . The secretary of education Ron Paige and the lieutenant governor will then take the podium to discuss education. . . . I do want to thank the folks at Booker Elementary for the hospitality. . . ."

The Raiders had to be in a panic. Where in the hell were 93 and 77? What the hell had gone wrong?

Or, maybe they already knew.

38

The tooth hanging on a chain around the neck of A.B. "Buzzy" Krongard came, according to legend, from a Great White that he had punched in the jaw. The shark's picture hangs in the office of the number-three man at CIA, who was appointed Executive Director in March 2001, six months prior to 911. According to Jeremy Scahill in his book *Blackwater*, Krongard was appointed after a career in which he was credited with building up one of America's oldest and most successful investment banking firms, Alex. Brown. Imagine the possibilities for a man with complete access to secret government intelligence and endless connections in stock and commodities trading.

A Princeton alum, an ex-Marine, a Hall of Fame lacrosse player and the legendary puncher of the Great White, Krongard was rumored to have been working with the CIA during his entire tenure with Alex. Brown. Scahill reported that the strange mix of high finance and CIA connections led Krongard to push for a new firm within the agency that would specialize in intelligence venture capitalism — in other words, a unit that could take real monetary bets on future trends and events, including, for example, the next big terrorist attack. And according to a former Blackwater executive, Buzzy Krongard and Erik Prince, Blackwater CEO, are "good buddies." In his book, Scahill reported that the first no-bid contract was handed to Blackwater from CIA through Buzzy Krongard in April 2002, a $5,400,000 no-bid deal to provide 20 security guards at the Kabul CIA station for six months. Krongard stated that he talked to Prince about the contract but couldn't remember who called whom and "was not sure which came first, the chicken or the egg."

But wait: Blackwater and the CIA are major players at Arizona's Pinal Airpark, the temporary home to dozens of Boeing airliners. The Blackwater CEO has his fleet of airplanes training at Pinal and now Buzzy Krongard is linked to a major worldwide investment firm. These connections came to the forefront when I encountered a series of strange stock trades involving United and American.

Anyone with foreknowledge of the 911 attacks would, of course, have had an opportunity to capitalize with trades in stocks and commodities futures. Either these hijackers were placing bets that they wouldn't be able to collect or someone damn close to the operation was parlaying inside information of the tactical plan.

The Wall Street Journal and the *San Francisco Chronicle* reported that on September 6th and 7th, "put" options speculating that United Airlines stock would go down were purchased through Deutschebank/ Alex. Brown, the same firm previously managed by Krongard. An enormous increase over normal sales activity placed 4,744 put options versus 396 "calls." On September 10th, 4,416 put options were purchased on American Airlines (compared with 748 calls), on the same day that Reuters reported airline stocks were poised to "take off." In both cases, the traders never cashed in the winnings and the FBI was unable to trace the amazingly insightful investors. No other airlines displayed these lopsided trading patterns. *The New York Times* reported that the head of the Alex. Brown unit of Deutschebank — which had its offices in the WTC — abruptly resigned from a $30 million, three-year contract on September 12, 2001.

The American exchanges that handle these trades, primarily the Chicago Board of Options Exchange (CBOE) and the NYSE, know on a daily basis what levels of put options are purchased. "Put options" are highly leveraged bets, tying up blocks of stock, that a given stock's share price will fall dramatically. To quote *60 Minutes* from September 19, 2001, "Sources tell *CBS News* that the afternoon before the attack, alarm bells were sounding over unusual trading in the U.S. stock options market." The transactions that week "could not have been planned and carried out without a certain knowledge, particularly heavy trading in oil and gold futures," said Germany's Bundesbank chief, Ernst Welke.

Unusual trading?

A jump in UAL put options above normal between September 6 and September 10, and 285 times higher than average on the Thursday before the attack.

A jump in American Airlines put options 60 times above normal on the day before the attacks. No similar trading occurred on any other airlines. [*Bloomberg Business Report*, the Institute for

Counterterrorism (ICT), Israel, citing data from the CBOE]

Morgan Stanley saw, between September 7 and 10, an increase of 27 times on put options on its shares. Merrill-Lynch saw a jump of more than 12 times the normal level of put options in the four trading days before the attacks. "This could very well be insider trading at the worst, most horrific, most evil use you've ever seen in your entire life. . . . This would be one of the most extraordinary coincidences in the history of mankind if it was a coincidence," said Dylan Ratigan of *Bloomberg Business News*, interviewed on *Good Morning Texas* on September 20.

"I saw put-call numbers higher than I've ever seen in 10 years of following the markets, particularly the options markets," said John Kinnucan, principal of Broadband Research. Jonathan Winer, an *ABC News* consultant, said, "It's absolutely unprecedented to see cases of insider trading covering the entire world from Japan, to the U.S., to North America, to Europe."

Andreas von Bülow, a former member of the German Parliament responsible for oversight of Germany's intelligence services, estimated the worldwide amount of the trading bets at $15 billion. *CBS News* gave a conservative estimate of $100 million.

Not a single U.S. or foreign investigative agency has announced any arrests or developments in the investigation of these trades, even though former Securities and Exchange Commission enforcement chief William McLucas told *Bloomberg News* that regulators would "certainly be able to track down every trade."

Britain's Financial Services Authority cleared bin Laden of insider trading while the Israeli Institute for Counter-Terrorism was the first entity to release a detailed report on the insider trading. So the same question returns: If it wasn't bin Laden, then who the hell was it?

Could Buzzy Krongard be to 911 what Ollie North was to Iran-Contra? Say it ain't so.

39

"Uhh . . . today, we've had a national tragedy." The president slowly pushed the words out as time moved into the fourth quarter of the attack window.

"Two airplanes have crashed into the World Trade Center . . . in an apparent terrorist attack on our country. I have spoken with Vice President Cheney, Governor Pataki, and the Director of the FBI and have ordered to pull resources of the federal government that will go to help the victims and their families . . ."

At 9:29: Tick . . . tick . . . tick . . .

". . . and conduct a full-scale investigation . . . to hunt down these folks . . . who committed this act. Terrorism against our nation will not stand. And now if you will join me in a moment of silence. . . ."

Tick . . . tick . . . tick . . .

George W. Bush bowed his head, as did the shocked children behind him, and held the silence for one, two, three, four, five seconds, enough time for American 77 to get closer, closer and closer to the capital. What he said next is not a misprint, but perhaps it was misspoken irony: "May God bless the victims of the families . . . and America." Then, with his best attempt at serious drama, he closed his folder and walked off the stage. Most in attendance were lost and seemed to think this was some sort of pep rally. The children cheered as he disappeared, again.

Meanwhile, American 77 was just popping up on the Capital ATC radar. "Hey, who is this guy?" The Langley fighters were still on the ground, waiting . . . waiting . . . .

40

Because multiple scenarios could have failed the Raiders' mission, a deep understanding of the entire airline system was required for success. The esoteric knowledge and sophistication involved rules out every known terrorist organization.

This tactical plan required a complicated scenario involving subtle intelligence on every front. For example, a good weather day was required for many reasons. September is the perfect month for big high pressure systems over the northeast U.S. and are easily forecast a week or more in advance. The evidence confirms that the mission went into "go" mode by September 5th, when a massive system of high pressure was forecast to be locked in place over the east coast for September 11th, and when the last of the hijackers' tickets were purchased. September 6th is also when the curious pattern of trading in airline stocks emerged.

Good weather helped the Raiders' chances in several areas of their time-critical tactical plan: First, good weather off the east coast combined with the early bank — meaning, the first morning scheduled departures — increased the chances of an on-time operation. Second, good weather would help the pilots see their targets. Absolutely great weather would enable them to see their targets from 40 miles out. Third, good weather would help keep the airliners' routes closer to the targets at the window for takeover times. Unstable weather with possible thunderstorms would increase the chance of being rerouted away to the north or to an unpredictable route. Good weather would insure that the Boston planes would be over New York's lower Hudson Valley at the perfect time. The normal good weather routes would place all planes in an ideal attack position. The likely deliberate choice of a period of exceptionally fine weather may indicate again how important it was to the Raiders that they create a simultaneous four-headed strike.

Finally comes a factor almost too weird to think about — unless you're possessed of a mind even more sinister than that of a jihadist terrorist. And that is, beautiful fall weather would produce images of destruction so vivid, so clear, we would never be able to forget them. Good weather supported the mission tactically but also may have supported it in a larger sense, if part of the plan was to make an everlasting impression for political impact.

41

Saudi pilot Hani Hanjour glided the American 757 down by the Flight Level Change method, slightly different than Jarrah's method on UA93. The sky was clear of clouds and, more importantly, after AA77 had taken a full 42 minutes to turn and fly back to the capital, clear of fighter jets.

With flight attendants and passengers screaming from the cabin, two pilots bleeding to death on the floor behind him and, almost certainly, blood covering his clothes and the instrument panel, he probably spotted the Pentagon from about 15 miles out. At 9:29 he leveled off at 7,000 feet and held 300 knots on the airspeed before clicking off the autopilot at 9:30. He proceeded to execute an absolutely perfect, descending 330-degree right turn. Without any undershoot or overshoot, he made a perfect rollout just five miles west of the Pentagon at an altitude of 2,500 feet with the target in the center windshield. He pushed the throttles to full power and pushed the yoke into a dive. The overspeed warnings began a continuous clack-clack-clack, and because he didn't disarm the Ground Proximity Warning System like Jarrah did, the GPWS screamed landing gear and flap warnings with a continuous and very loud series of "WHOOP! WHOOP! TOO LOW! WHOOP! WHOOP! PULL UP! WHOOP! WHOOP! TOO LOW! PULL UP!" The airspeed raced from 300 to 350 to 400 to 450 until he impacted at 460 knots indicated airspeed, or 530 miles per hour. Just before the impact, he had leveled the plane five feet off the ground for a perfect torpedo shot on the 90-foot west wall of America's military headquarters. I have 15,000 hours in heavy jets, and I would have a damn hard time matching that performance, even in a peaceful setting. But Hani Hanjour, a novice pilot from the same hometown as Prince Bandar, was in total control of the aircraft as he generated a 200-foot fireball and killed 189 people. Was it a missile? Yes, a Boeing 757 missile.

Mysteriously, the plane hit the heart of the American military at 9:38, one hour and fifteen minutes after Boston Center knew that American 11 was hijacked and a full hour after the north tower was hit. The Andrews F-16s remained on the ground, just seconds away by air; the Langley F-16s had just lifted off but were heading east out over the Atlantic, on a bogus heading for reasons that would take a full day of hearings to explain. Hani Hanjour might have been more than a half hour late on the tactical plan but miraculously, in terms of hitting the target, it made no difference. In the coming months, when the Redskins or any other NFL team within our borders needed a spectacular flyover to coincide with the National Anthem before kickoff, those F-16s would hit it perfectly on the last refrain. And the crowd, many with tears in their eyes, would cheer wildly.

Across the Potomac, at the Executive Office Building, visitors had been told to evacuate the area. One of these visitors was standing on the street just across from the White House at 9:35. She noticed a big white airplane orbiting in the clear blue over the city. She decided to snap a picture of the plane with her Pentax camera.

And also out of the blue, here's a question: Why in the world, in less than 48 hours, would Prince Bandar and the Commander-in-Chief be smoking cigars together on the White House balcony while the Pentagon was still smoldering across the Potomac?

42

Those cigars on the Truman balcony on September 13, 2001 symbolized a political alliance between George W. Bush and Prince Bandar that began, as Bob Woodward describes it in *State of Denial*, when Governor Bush of Texas began seriously planning his eventual run for the presidency in 1997. Bandar's dear friend, the former president, prevailed upon him to pay his son a visit.

According to Woodward, Bush said to the prince, "My dad told me before I make up my mind, go and talk to Bandar. One, he's our friend. . . . Number two, he knows everyone around the world who counts. And number three, he will give you his view on what he sees happening in the world. Maybe he can set up meetings for you with people around the world."

Bandar quickly and even brutally schooled W in the ways of real world politics, dismissing any remaining concerns the first-term governor might have about needing to be dishonest:

> "Never mind if you really want to be honest. . . . If you really want to stick to that, just enjoy this term and go do something fun. In the big boys' game, it's cutthroat, it's bloody and it's not pleasant."

Then, according to Woodward, "Bandar changed the subject." Bandar said that while Bush had been flying F-102s in Texas, he too had been in Texas, flying F-102s at Perrin Air Force Base.

"Remember," Bandar said, "what they taught you. . . ."

> Keep your eye on the ball. When I am flying that jet and my life is on the line, and I pick up that enemy aircraft, I don't care if everything around me dies. I will keep my eye on that aircraft, and I will do whatever it takes. *I'll never take my eye off.*

We can only wonder which enemy aircraft Bandar had ever picked up, but, anyway, two weeks after 911, in an interview with Lowell Bergman of PBS, and speaking of the United States, Bandar was reminded by Bergman that "we're not a monarchy."

"And maybe you regret it," Bandar retorted, "that you are not a monarchy. Maybe if you were a monarchy, you would have more common sense to do the right thing. And not get too carried away with quote-unquote 'freedom'."

There's little wonder why the Bushes love their Bandar.

43

Just as the Pentagon was being hit, CNN's John King reported seeing, and CNN cameras caught a glimpse of, a "big white plane" circling the area of the Capitol. It was the same big white plane the visitor had snapped with her Pentax.

The 911 Commissioners would later get the testimony of NORAD's General Larry Arnold. He made a remarkable statement that made investigators consider filing perjury charges against him with the Justice Department. Arnold described his responses from Tyndall Air Base on the Florida panhandle.

"It was our intent to intercept United 93. And in fact, my own staff, we were orbiting now over Washington, D.C., by this time, and I was personally anxious to see what 93 was going to do, and our intent was to intercept it. . . . The brave men and women who took over that aircraft prevented us from making the awful decision," the general testified somberly.

But when the 911 Commissioners reviewed the military response to United 93, they determined that NORAD was notified by the FAA only after United 93 had crashed. And the only plane "orbiting . . . over Washington" was the plane John King had mentioned and that would later appear with great clarity in the Pentax shot. In 2007, around the anniversary of 911, CNN ran a piece about this "mystery" plane, as did the Discovery Channel, and showed its film again. The interesting implication is that General Arnold may not have been lying.

The photograph clearly shows a four-engine, swept-wing Boeing, with a large hump starting from the cockpit and ending about halfway aft. There's another smaller hump on top of the larger hump. It doesn't take a 747 captain to easily identify the plane as a Boeing 747, except maybe it would take one to determine that it was at about 15,000 feet. The plane is painted white with a blue stripe down the center of the fuselage with an American flag on the large familiar tail.

The smaller hump is a special modification known to have been made for NORAD's highly advanced reconnaissance plane, called the E4-B. Within that smaller hump is a satellite tracking system that would indeed allow General Arnold "to see what United 93 was going to do."

But if he could see United 93 at 274 miles out, he could surely see American 77 approaching right beneath his big white plane. In fact, he could have seen all of the Raiders' attacks, in real time, from Boston to Washington to way out over Pennsylvania.

Later in the day, George Walker Bush stated that he "saw the airplane hit the World Trade Center" and said that he thought it was just "a terrible pilot." But video of American 11 hitting the tower wasn't released until the next day. When American 11 hit the north tower, the president was inside his limo. Perhaps he simply misspoke, but perhaps he could have cleared this up for us with a little testimony under oath. Would it be too much to ask? It's really . . . important.

Because the mystery plane has been positively identified as General Arnold's "orbiting" E4-B, the obvious questions are difficult to ask without adding some sort of profanity. If General Arnold could see American 77 approaching, why didn't he notify the fighters at Langley or right below at Andrews and give them vectors to intercept?

In typical White House fashion, they have refused even to discuss the plane's existence. Forget testifying under oath. Who's going to make them?

General Arnold has since retired.

44

An official inquiry into any vital failure of the United States intelligence and defense should come as a matter of course. But after 911, a wall of resistance was thrown up by the Bush Administration, with Vice President Cheney in the lead. Helped by continually manufactured distractions of new terror alerts, Anthrax scares and a "global war on terror" — distractions promoted daily by American news organizations — the administration succeeded in fending off a serious look at the compiled evidence for more than a year. President Bush's promise on the morning of September 11 "to conduct a full-scale investigation to hunt down these folks who committed this act," proved hollow.

The 911 Commission wasn't formed until 2003. Philip Shenon, the *New York Times* reporter assigned to cover the Commission's investigation, in 2007 published *The Commission: The Uncensored History of the 9/11 Investigation*, which documents the stonewalling and undermining endured by the 911 Commission from the Executive Branch during the entire investigation.

As Shenon relates, the Commission staff was capable and dedicated in its investigation, and the basic first steps were executed competently, with the collection of thousands of pages of records and reports. The Commission's co-chairs, Thomas Kean and Lee Hamilton, tried to keep this supremely important project free from politics and to maintain a high level of integrity. They would later confess that they were unable to overpower the White House. As they wrote in their book *Without Precedent*, the Commission had been designed to fail.

The one clear constant in White House behavior on the entire subject of 911, before, during and after, is inaction. There was no action to alert the concerned parties, such as the airlines, before the attack, despite dozens of warnings. There was no meaningful action to stop the attack as it was occurring — to scramble every fighter jet on the east coast and give them shootdown authority. There was no action to give the 911 Commission anything like the subpoena power it needed to get to the truth. With the aid of then White House counsel Alberto Gonzalez, the prime actors in the failure were able to set the ground rules for their own interrogation and testimony. The man who had most failed in America's defense was able to demand an interrogation without an oath and without any record, including handwritten notes.

The most effective roadblock to justice turned out to be the placement of Philip Zelikow as the 911 Commission's Executive Director. Zelikow was a former member of the National Security Council for the first President Bush, co-author of a political book with Condoleezza Rice, a member of the Bush transition team and, incredibly, the author of the policy paper that the White House used to justify a preemptive American invasion of Iraq — authorship that Zelikow and the White House obscured from Kean and Hamilton. The highly competent 911 Commission staff described Zelikow as a "White House mole." In keeping with that role, and despite the fact that he had promised not to communicate with the people he was investigating, Zelikow maintained secret daily contact with Karl Rove (as confirmed by phone records) as he controlled the final edit of the report. In short, the White House was successful in planting a loyal member of the neoconservative, pro-war group into the position where he could and would change the entire face of the evidence.

The phone records show nearly daily calls to Rove and to Rice during the time when evidence was beginning to reveal a solid relationship between the hijackers and high levels of the Saudi government, including Prince Bandar, who was financing the team that later commandeered and crashed American Flight 77 into the Pentagon.

This and other Saudi evidence was abundant and damning, but it never saw the light of day under Zelikow. Gone was the evidence of a direct line between the 911 terrorists and the government of Saudi Arabia that the congressional investigators had uncovered before the forming of the commission. Twenty-eight pages of report revealing that Saudi officials had known that terrorists were entering the U.S. in preparation for an attack were blacked out. According to Florida Senator Bob Graham, it was indisputable that Saudi spies under the direction of Saudi officials were supporting the hijackers. Senator Graham believed that the White House was determined to cover up Saudi involvement and had found an eager accomplice in FBI Director Robert Mueller, who had once been instrumental in botching the BCCI investigation. Mueller, Senator Graham believed, was "directly involved in the effort to hide the truth."

Critical evidence was dug up by the joint congressional staff director Eleanor Hill, a veteran congressional investigator, and Michael Jacobson, a former FBI lawyer and counterterrorism analyst who had joined the staff and was one of its most reliable and dogged investigators. Buried in FBI files was the documentation of two Saudi hijackers, Nawaf al-Hazmi and Khalid al-Mihdhar, who had entered the U.S. in January 2000. The CIA had been following the duo as they traveled to Asia before arriving in Los Angeles; the CIA said it had alerted the FBI once these two entered the country. The FBI claims that there is no record of that warning.

Jacobson discovered that the two hijackers were befriended soon after their arrival by Omar Bayoumi, a smooth-talking Saudi on the payroll of Dallah Avco, the aviation contractor with ties to Prince Bandar and the Saudi government. Bayoumi spent most of his days at a mosque in El Cajon, about 15 miles outside of San Diego, as a ghost employee on a steady salary of around $3,000 per month. A $40,000 increase for Bayoumi came after the arrival of the two hijackers; thousands more dollars were funneled through another Saudi spy named Osama Bassan. The congressional investigators were surprised to learn that much of the money was traced to the account of Saudi Prince Bandar, whose private Airbus A-340 was often seen at Lindbergh Field in San Diego during this period prior to the attacks. Bandar also had meetings with Donald Rumsfeld, who gave him a private tour of the Pentagon on February 5, 2001, less than a month after the inauguration and seven months prior to the attack.

With funds from Prince Bandar's cashier's checks, Bayoumi assisted the hijackers in finding an apartment, opening checking accounts and obtaining driver's licenses and Social Security numbers. He organized a party in San Diego to welcome them to America before the two began making car trips to Las Vegas and

Arizona in the year prior to the attacks. The congressional investigators were shocked to learn that a longtime FBI informant, Abdussattar Shaikh, had also housed the hijackers for a time at his own home.

After Jacobson learned of this connection, the FBI blocked the investigators from interviewing the informant who had had the terrorists living under his nose — and all of this evidence was omitted by Zelikow from the Commission report. The White House had threatened the investigators with prison sentences if they continued down this path; the FBI began a criminal investigation on the leaking of "classified information." Vice President Cheney began making a series of calls to Senator Graham and others with threats and vows to "terminate our assistance" to the committee.

After the attacks, Bayoumi told FBI agents an improbable tale about how he had met the two hijackers in a food mart in Los Angeles right after a scheduled meeting at the Saudi consulate. Later evidence showed that the consulate meeting was with Saudi diplomat Fahad al-Thumairy, who would later be interviewed by the 911 Commissioners in Riyadh. Jacobson found a larger network of support for the hijackers including an Arabic-speaking driver for al-Thumairy and his contacts. The Tunisian driver was shown a series of photographs of young Arab men and quickly picked out the two hijackers.

The Commission sent members to interview Omar Bayoumi in October 2003; he had retreated to Saudi Arabia after intense scrutiny from FBI agents. He told the commissioners that he knew al-Thumairy but talked with him only about religious matters, although he had driven from San Diego to Los Angeles to meet him in 2000.

In the Riyadh interview, al-Thumairy appeared hostile to the United States. He began by answering questions through an interpreter, but when the questions became accusatory, he answered in English. Jacobson began to focus on his relationship with Bayoumi and al-Thumairy claimed that he did not know Bayoumi. That's when they produced telephone records that documented dozens of calls beginning in December 1998. Evidence that the attacks went into a "go" mode just as George W. Bush was declared president is indicated by a spike in calls between Bayoumi and al-Thumairy in December 2000.

In the final report of the 911 Commission, Philip Zelikow was unwilling to mention these Saudi spies, who were connected to an aviation firm connected to Prince Bandar, who was directly connected to George W. Bush, who refused to take decisive action before, during and after attacks that ended up providing a pretext to propel the United States into a preemptive war with Iraq according to a doctrine that had been written by — Philip Zelikow. Instead he concluded that the sworn enemies of Saudi Prince Bandar, al-Qaeda, without any evidence of aviation expertise or the planning and training that they would have needed, had somehow foiled every element of national security and killed three thousand people in the heart of New York and at the heart of the American military in the nation's capital, surrounded by military fighter bases.

One of the most effective maneuvers to distort the truth is the absence, in Zelikow's final report, of an accurate timeline for the morning of 911. The testimony of key players was proven to be distorted, perhaps deliberately, including that of Air Force General Larry Arnold, who would produce more questions than he would answer.

When the 911 Commission staff and its investigators uncovered the gross negligence of the administration, Zelikow went into cover-up mode, while those who had been incompetent in defending the nation ran campaign ads to frighten voters. Dick Cheney let it be known that voting for Democrats would increase the chances of another terrorist attack — while the Commission staff was discovering a complete breakdown of protocol in the defense of America.

But Zelikow was keeping all of this evidence under wraps as a fake bin Laden video was released just a week before the 2004 presidential election. This was one of three fake tapes that were used in a ridiculous reinvention of bin Laden, a new darker Santa Claus lurking behind every Terror Alert, the symbol of evil created by the very people who slipped the Commission the tales of the deranged KSM without any accounting for how the attack was planned or developed.

The evidence against Bandar was hidden in the final report because Zelikow argued that it was not conclusive. Yet, thirdhand unverifiable testimony from KSM, the most obscurely sourced of all of the Commission's evidence, was central to its conclusions. Hard evidence on the Saudis was excluded, and shaky testimony of KSM used to explain the entire plot. The phraseology of the Commission's acceptance of this testimony is hauntingly similar to the phraseology of the media's meek, virtually automatic acceptance of the alleged Osama bin Laden tapes.

One alternative explanation for the omissions and distortions in the report would be gross incompetence and ineptitude. However, considering all the evidence, and especially considering the continuous call for war and the deliberate use of all possible means to achieve that war, by the same people who were being investigated, incompetence is virtually ruled out. The Zelikow-led final report was, in the end, a cover-up.

One excellent indication that something must have gone terribly wrong: The Saudis lauded the Commission findings and posted them all over the walls of their embassy in Washington. When pressed, Prince Bandar quotes the report by heart, and quickly points out that the FBI cleared them of any wrongdoing.

45

Five days after the attacks, on September 16, 2001, Vice President Cheney would somberly tell the story of having made the toughest decision of that past Tuesday, in an interview with Tim Russert from Camp David. Referring to the decision to order fighter jets to shoot down passenger planes that were approaching Washington, Cheney said, "Well, I suppose the toughest decision was this question of whether or not we would intercept incoming commercial aircraft."

Russert followed up: "And you decided. . . ."

"We decided to do it" — referring to himself and the president.

Russert: "So if the United States government became aware that a hijacked commercial airliner was destined for the White House or the Capitol, we would take the plane down?"

"Yes," said the somber White House veteran. "The president made the decision on my recommendation." Cheney said that Bush had relayed the decision to Cheney in one of their telephone calls that morning.

"Now, people say, you know, that's a horrendous decision to make," he continued. "Well, it is."

Unfortunately, as even the Commission report makes clear (if you make the extra effort to connect the dots), Cheney was lying.

No shootdown authorization was ever passed to the pilots flying at NORAD's direction. By 10:45 A.M., however, another set of fighters was circling Washington under entirely different rules of engagement. These fighters, part of the 113th Wing of the District of Columbia Air National Guard, launched out of Andrews Air Force Base in Maryland in response to information passed to them, not by the White House, but by the Secret Service. The first of these fighters was airborne at 10:38, over 30 minutes after the last plane had crashed.

As the Commission report states: "General David Wherley—the commander of the 113th Wing—reached out to the Secret Service . . . . The guidance for Wherley was to send up the aircraft, with orders to protect the White House and take out any aircraft that threatened the Capitol. General Wherley translated this in military terms to flying 'weapons free' — that is, the decision to shoot rests in the cockpit, or in this case in the cockpit of the lead pilot. He passed these instructions to the pilots. . . ."

A Secret Service agent said he was getting authorization from Cheney. However, the Commission added the following:

"The President and the Vice President indicated to us they had not been aware that fighters had been scrambled out of Andrews, at the request of the Secret Service and outside the military chain of command. There is no evidence that NORAD headquarters or military officials . . . knew — during the morning of September 11 — that the Andrews planes were airborne and operating under different rules of engagement."

Cheney's solemn statement to a stunned nation on Meet the Press was that he and the president had decided to shoot down incoming airliners. However, the White House records every incoming or outgoing phone call. Seven logs were kept on the Cheney–Bush calls on 911. The Situation Room keeps one. The Secret Service keeps one. The White House switchboard keeps one. Four separate logs were kept by military officers working in the White House. There were seven separate logs chronicling the length, the time, the subject and all pertinent information for the calls between Cheney and Bush. There was no evidence on any of the logs that a shootdown was even discussed, much less authorized. When the vice president said, "The president made the decision on my recommendation," it was a lie.

The only documented mention of even the possibility of a shootdown order was in Scooter Libby's notes, between 10:15 and 10:18 A.M. His note read: "Aircraft 60 miles out, confirmed a hijack — engage? VP? JB [Josh Bolton]: Get President and confirm engage order." This may have been one of the earliest post-attack deception tactics; everyone on the Raider side knew that UA93, the last of the four, had crashed ten minutes earlier.

NORAD records indicate that it wasn't until between 10:14 and 10:19 that messages from a lieutenant colonel at the White House were being sent that Cheney had confirmed fighters were cleared to engage inbound aircraft if they could verify the aircraft was hijacked. However, the order was not passed along because the NORAD commander knew that such an order could not come from the Vice President; he knew that it had to follow protocol: from the President to the Secretary of Defense to the combatant commander. This order was useless and Cheney, a former Secretary of Defense, must have known that it was an invalid order.

The Andrews squadron's "weapons free" authorization came 40 minutes after United 93 had crashed. The impact of the U.S. military defense was exactly the same as if there had been no U.S. military defense at all. The Raiders' tactical plan either displayed an uncanny inside knowledge of our military readiness or relied on inaction by our Commander-in-Chief, or both.

46

In asserting that there is much more to 911 than the official story would have us believe, and that responsibility must lie with a group or groups other than al-Qaeda, I have focused mostly on two of the three classic criteria usually involved in establishing guilt. Out of the triad of "means, motive and opportunity," the evidence we have been discussing pertains to means — the physical and logistical ability to carry out these attacks — and to opportunity — the circumstances that made the attacks possible at a certain place and time. We have touched on motive only indirectly.

For any persons wishing to execute such an attack and blame it on al-Qaeda, a highly plausible motive makes the terrorist group an ideal scapegoat. Never mind that no one has even tried to explain in any detail how al-Qaeda managed to do it; the situation is very much as if you wanted to murder your neighbor Bob and pin it on crazy Fred at the end of the street, who has been threatening for years to do Bob in. When Bob is finally killed, if you play your cards right, who's going to believe it wasn't Fred? Al-Qaeda has expressed hostility to the U.S. and is accused in attacks on our embassies in Africa and the *U.S.S. Cole* in Yemen.

In looking at the possible responsibility of any other group, it will be understandably very difficult for many Americans to consider, even for an instant, that this attack could have been planned and directed by other Americans. Even with my background in "black operations" — black operations under the direction of Vice President Bush, no less — I still had some hope, at first, that my darkest suspicions might evaporate in the strong light of the evidence. These would be unthinkable black ops indeed. My fear now is that they may not be over.

It is impossible to know to what lengths people will go for power — we won't know until we get the facts, meaning, all the facts. 911, had it succeeded — that is, had it produced the intended near-simultaneous four-headed strike — could have generated political power for at least an entire generation.

If we grant the hypothesis that 911 may have been an ultimate case of dirty tricks, a sucker punch designed to deceive the world, and to grab power, it is worth examining who gained power as a result and then how they used it. The short answer, of course, would be the Bush Administration, which used fear and hysteria to consolidate more and still more power. If part of the purpose was to push war with Iraq, then we have to address the big pink elephant in the living room, the one behind Bandar's cigar smoke rings: the oceans of black gold that lie beneath the Iraqi and Iranian sands.

In May 2001, Dick Cheney delivered the National Energy Policy report to President Bush, a report that had been shaped by the work of Cheney's energy task force, led by our friend James Baker. The Baker task force produced a report, "Strategic Energy Policy Challenges for the 21st Century," in April 2001.

According to the Baker report, Saddam Hussein became a swing oil producer by turning Iraq's oil taps "on and off" whenever he felt it was in his interest to do so. During these periods Saudi Arabia stepped up to the plate and provided replacement oil supplies to the market. Hussein, the report says, used his own "export program to manipulate oil markets." The report's implications are clear: the national energy security of the U.S. was now in the hands of an open adversary and the Saudis might not make up the difference in the future. The Baker report recommends: "The United States should conduct an immediate policy review of Iraq, including military, energy, economic and political/diplomatic assessments. . . . Sanctions that are not effective should be phased out and replaced with highly focused and enforced sanctions that target the regime's ability to maintain and acquire weapons of mass destruction." Military intervention is listed as a viable option.

When Vice President Cheney handed the official national report to President Bush, the cabinet members who formed the National Energy Policy Development Group were listed as its authors. A closer look reveals that the Baker report was the mainframe. In the end, almost every major policy action in the Baker report was incorporated in the national report

By December 2002, an "independent working group" led by ambassadors Edward P. Djerejian and Frank G. Wisner wrote a guide for the president that described American actions after an Iraq war. They had created a "perfect" war on paper: The war was presumed to have occurred. It was a fast, smooth war. It ended nicely. There were no complications.

Titled "Guiding Principles for U.S. Post-Conflict Policy in Iraq," the report was cosponsored by the Council on Foreign Relations and the James A. Baker III Institute for Public Policy of Rice University. Addressing the motives of the U.S., the report warns the president, "Western anti-war activists, the Arab public, average Iraqis and international media have all accused the United States of planning an attack on Iraq not to dismantle weapons of mass destruction but as a camouflaged plan to 'steal' Iraq's oil for the sake of American oil interests." The solution: any repairs, future investments, oil exports and sales of oil must be made transparent and involve both international and Iraqi oversight.

The report then gets down to the nitty-gritty. "Iraq has the second largest proven oil reserves in the world (behind Saudi Arabia) estimated at 112 billion barrels with as many as 220 billion barrels of resources deemed probable. Of Iraq's 74 discovered and evaluated oil fields, only 15 have been developed." In the western desert "there are 526 known structures that have been discovered, delineated, mapped, and classified as potential prospects in Iraq, of which only 125 have been drilled." This is the mother lode. To hell with going green when there's another oil kingdom to be enjoyed. Occupation of Iraq would be a major step to the new oil kingdom that the Bush family had pursued since leaving Connecticut for the rich oilfields of west Texas in 1951.

But great American dynasties apparently cannot live by oil alone; to ensure the greatest wealth and consolidate it, even into the furthest imaginable future generation, they need power. In the pursuit of power, the destinies of George W. Bush, a small group of American so-called "neoconservatives" and the Saudi royal family, fronted by Prince Bandar, became intertwined.

At the end of the Gulf War in 1991, the U.S. decided it was too risky to invade Baghdad or attempt an occupation, even though there were nearly one million coalition troops and contractors in the sand. This decision came over loud objections from Prince Bandar, who would remain upset for 13 years, until his friend's son finally attempted the occupation, but with fewer than two hundred thousand troops.

Also among the discontents in 1991 were the neoconservative future members of something that called itself Project for a New American Century, or PNAC. PNAC co-founder William Kristol, Richard Perle, Donald Rumsfeld and others were screaming for a push into Baghdad.

Then the oil seekers in Washington were out of office for eight years, during the presidency of Bill Clinton. George Bush had been fired by the American voters after one term and a dismal approval rating, despite a temporary spike during the Gulf War. One thing was certain: The fall from power by the Baker-Bush team was going to be corrected; a detailed plan for that purpose was taking shape during the Clinton years.

In 1998 members of PNAC, including Donald Rumsfeld and Paul Wolfowitz, wrote to President Clinton urging him to remove Saddam Hussein from power using U.S. diplomatic, political and military power. The letter argued that Saddam would pose a threat to the United States and its Middle East allies and oil resources in the region, if he succeeded in maintaining his alleged stockpile of weapons of mass destruction. The letter also argued that an Iraq war would be justified by Hussein's defiance of UN containment and his persistent threat to U.S. interests.

A key PNAC document, and the intellectual centerpiece for neoconservative foreign policy, written in 2000, is titled "Rebuilding America's Defenses." The group argues that the United States must be prepared to take military action and that the year 2000 deployment of forces is obsolete. Defense spending and force deployment should go toward placing forces at new permanent military bases in Southeast Europe and Southwest Asia, to shape security in critical regions of the world. After identifying "hostile regimes" as Iraq, North Korea, Iran and Syria, the authors advocate the radical new doctrine of the preemptive use of force: "The history of the 20th Century should have taught us that it is important to shape circumstances before crises emerge and to meet threats before they become dire." Truly, PNAC was a think tank for creating the Post-911 World.

The signers included a who's who of the future administration, such as Dick Cheney, Donald Rumsfeld, Paul Wolfowitz, Lewis Libby and Richard Armitage, plus Jeb Bush and others.

PNAC's writings were not the only papers influencing the Bush presidency as it assumed power in 2001. Other reports from conservative think tanks like Stanford's Hoover Institution, the American Enterprise Institute and the Heritage Foundation had the ears of those who favored using America's great military power to carve out an empire and keep America on a course of global domination.

The Council on Foreign Relations, advising the new president in June 2001, stated, "Saddam Hussein and his regime pose a growing danger to the Middle East and the United States. The regime cannot be rehabilitated. Therefore, the goal of regime replacement should remain a fundamental tenet of U.S. policy options." This paper advises the president there are three red lines that Saddam Hussein might possibly cross. If he crosses any one of them, we will gain the support of the Arabs and the Turks against him: "First, Iraqi military threats or attacks on allied forces. Second, Iraqi threats or attacks on neighboring states. Third, Iraqi acquisition and deployment of weapons of mass destruction or their use, including nuclear, chemical and biological weapons." This sounds like a rough draft for George W. Bush's dire warnings in the 2003 State of the Union Address.

But how do these statements point directly to a motive for 911? They don't. For that, we must go to a little-remarked passage in the PNAC manifesto. The passage is extraordinary, and, in the context of all that has happened, chilling.

After making their recommendations, the authors warn that "the process of transformation, even if it brings revolutionary change, is likely to be a long one, absent some catastrophic and catalyzing event — like a new Pearl Harbor."

Conclusion: False Flag 911

" . . . Some catastrophic and catalyzing event — like a new Pearl Harbor." Did some person or persons decide that if a new Pearl Harbor wasn't going to happen all by itself, they would arrange one? Did they foresee — agreeing with PNAC — that if this could be arranged, and their role hidden, it could lead to a new neoconservative century, with pro-war majorities guaranteed for many election cycles to come, and an open-ended license to march through the oil-rich Middle East, to Iraq and then Iran?

The evidence examined here, compiled by many focused investigators, calls for a real inquiry. It would be the first honest inquiry into what really happened on September 11, 2001.

Evidence suggests that 911 was a classic "false flag" attack — probably the bloodiest, most horrendous, and most cynical false flag gambit in world history. The most celebrated perpetrator of false flag incidents was, no surprise, Adolf Hitler, as when he ordered the burning of Germany's parliament building, the Reichstag, in 1933 and blamed it on the communists in order to dramatically enhance his power. This was only brought to light by documents obtained by the Allies after the war and by testimony at the Nuremberg trials. Hitler and his lieutenant Reinhard Heydrich used a false flag attack to justify the Nazi aggression that triggered the Second World War. The Gleiwitz incident on August 31, 1939, was staged to look like a Polish attack on a German radio station. Later in 1939, Stalin used a false flag simulation of a Finnish attack to justify attacking Finland.

But false flag attacks are hardly limited to dictatorships. The mysterious explosion of the *U.S.S. Maine* in 1898, the immediate pretext for the Spanish-American War, has long been thought not to have been Spanish sabotage, as claimed at the time, but a false flag attack arranged either by the U.S. government or by American newspapers eager for war.

In 1953, the U.S. and Britain orchestrated Operation Ajax, a false flag propaganda operation against the democratically elected leader of Iran, Mohammed Mosaddeq. Information regarding the CIA-sponsored coup has been largely declassified and is available in the CIA archives.

In 1962 Operation Northwoods was planned by the U.S. Department of Defense to spark a war with Cuba; it involved a scenario to hijack a passenger plane and blame it on Cuba. It was authored by the Joint Chiefs of Staff, nixed by John F. Kennedy, and finally came to light through the Freedom of Information Act.

As for the North Vietnamese attacks in the Gulf of Tonkin in 1964, whatever happened, it wasn't strictly a false flag. But its many now undisputed false elements should prove cautionary concerning what is possible in our democracy.

It has hardly been noticed in the hysteria surrounding 911, but this was ultimately an attack that failed. Through its two key tactical failures, the delay of American 77 and the extended tragedy of United 93, it failed to achieve its real strategic goal. The element of surprise — complete surprise, across the board — was to have been the key to its success as a truly long-term, world-changing event. If the plan had been executed perfectly, the footprints of the tactical planners may have never been discovered. 'If' being the operative word.

If they had all struck at once, the disposition of the fighter jets would never have come into play. There would be no conversation about the shootdown orders that weren't given, the bizarre hiding and delaying inside the classroom, the NORAD responses, the E4-B orbiting the capital before the Pentagon was hit, Cheney making the "horrible decision" that he didn't actually make, the odd testimony of General Arnold, and on and on. They all could have said — and I believe they were supposed to be able to say — "Gee, it was over before we could do anything." Over by 9:11 on 911.

Iraq was the first target planned for preemptive war, employing a rationale written by Philip Zelikow, who was inserted as the Executive Director of the 911 Commission and who distorted our picture of the attacks. That picture replaced Saudis working for Prince Bandar with a new set of suspects, suspects who, curiously, have yet to be charged by the FBI with 911, but who have long been convicted in the public and media mind.

We know by now that we have been lied to on every front.

First we went to Iraq because of WMD, then it was to get Saddam, then for democracy, now it's for stability. In fact, we are there to get the oil; period, the end. The lies that led us into war have all been thoroughly documented by others. What's missing is the full horror of the story — the opening chapter, 911. Unfortunately, the lies did not just start with Iraq. The pattern of this administration has been nothing if not consistent: cynicism, deception, brutal self-serving manipulation. September 11th itself may prove to be the most massive, most incredible blunder within a parade of calamities, not just America's nightmare but by far the blackest episode in American political history. And all for the sake of driving an unprecedented retreat from democracy.

There is a way out of this disaster, and that is our system of justice. If we truly want liberty and justice for all, there is work to be done. This is our duty as American citizens. As Prince Bandar himself once remarked, although perhaps with something different in mind, freedom isn't free.

The mainframe of evidence for a real inquiry into 911 has already been built. Honest Americans who worked on our behalf as congressional investigators, 911 Commission staff, FBI agents, CIA officers, former administration officials, FAA and NTSB investigators, have all contributed to the abundant credible evidence needed to start the inquiry. All that is needed are witnesses to testify under oath. The easiest way to get this accomplished is to demand action by our representatives in Washington, a simple letter to our respective senators and congressman, for starters. Our letters should simply ask for hearings on the 911 evidence and demand that no witness be excused from testifying under oath for any reason. It's not too late to take the evidence and hand it to an independent and bipartisan commission with subpoena power.

This would be a bloodless and legal revolution. It may not be as exciting for some as a war, but it might restore our democracy.

The situation is grave. The 911 Raiders remain at large. In the 2008 election year the entire Republican campaign has focused on the old distorted fears, from gay marriage to the old spectre of 911. Election year Octobers have been proven to be prime time for unpleasant surprises, and we can only wonder where Bandar Bush's A340 may be headed at the moment. One problem with the failure of 911 to create a durable conservative majority, thanks to the dismal performance of the administration, is that the Raiders may now feel pressured to try again, and this time up the ante, maybe even lighting off a nuclear dirty bomb to reintroduce the fear and hysteria needed for the New American Century's plan for permanent war. Can we ante up the action needed to prevent further catastrophe?

You tell me. Please write your three letters today.

Postscript: Wall Street II

On September 10, 2001, a corporate revolution was in progress. The employees of United Airlines had begun to bypass the Wall Street players. Led by members of the Airline Pilots Association through a long and difficult struggle, in 1994 they had gained control of the company from the investment banks. The battle of lawyers and bankers was a tooth-and-nail affair that few Americans could see, but with billions of dollars at stake. Now United was a promising new prototype of the American corporation. Employees felt confident that they had finally brought an end to insider deals that siphoned hard-earned profits into shell corporations and sweetheart bonuses.

The pilots had led a fight in the 1980s, during the first Bush Administration, when corporate raiders were bidding on the airline with the intention of splitting off its assets and selling them piecemeal. The pilots mounted their own bid in defense and drove the threat away. With Bush 41's re-election defeat, and changes at the Department of Labor, it became possible for the pilots and mechanics to relight their effort to take United into a stock ownership plan, using 25 percent of future salaries and another 10 percent in future retirement funds. The result was 55% ownership in UAL Corporation and seats on the board of directors. By 2001, the employees had turned the company around with logic and efficiency. Performance reports and customer satisfaction were at all-time highs. Employees felt that their careers were secure; retirement and health care benefits led the industry. The proud people who built and operated the airline were all heavily invested in their own performance. Passengers raved about the turnaround in service and a fresh new energy circled the world via the industry's greatest fleet, through its top-ranked hubs. The success of the Employee Stock Ownership Plan (ESOP) offered a new model to employees of other large American corporations. At United, the future was bright. On Wall Street, the bankers were bitter.

By September 10, 2008, United Airlines will teeter on its second bankruptcy in seven years. Because of the attacks on United airplanes and employees on 911, UAL stock fell, as some strangely insightful investors had foreseen, from $80 a share until it was worthless paper. The first blood shed on 911 was that of airline pilots, who had trusted that government intelligence would at the very least keep us informed of major security threats. Four United ALPA pilots were murdered with knives across their throats and lay dying as their planes were crashed and their passengers killed in an attack blamed on foreign terrorists.

The Bush Administration spoke about saving the airlines while promoting exactly the opposite result. They formed the ATSB, or Airline Transportation Stabilization Board, announcing it as a compassionate move toward the United and American employees. In reality, the board was three political appointees whose only advice was for the employees to take massive pay and benefit cuts — before they spun United into bankruptcy court. All labor agreements were shredded as Wall Street regained control of the company and reissued new stock with a new symbol. The employees lost all of their investments and have been excluded from the new board. Retirement funds have all been terminated. Pilot salaries have been slashed by over fifty percent. The company leads the airline industry in customer complaints. Health care benefits have been slashed. Changes to working conditions have been draconian and morale is at an all-time low. Crew are searched at the same TSA checkpoints as passengers. ALPA's Wall Street enemies are back in total control, with their very own former oil industry CEO, who, after "leading" United through bankruptcy by slashing employee compensation, compensated himself with a $43 million bonus — a slap in the face to all who had sacrificed to survive the federal bankruptcy. Many employees find their homes in foreclosure, having been unable to keep pace with sinking salaries and rising costs. Oil companies now regulate United's fleet plan and control its profits through a spiraling oil market. No further major corporations have converted to employee ownership. Across America, oil companies swim in record profits as the middle class sinks in red ink.

Veteran pilots can look back to the days of great airline men, when the CEO would roam the airline, speaking with all the employees and lifting morale. Those days are gone. Most United employees have never seen their leader as he focuses on the bottom-line numbers that he believes are all that count. Sadly, he's an all too typical CEO in a new world of sweet stock options and golden parachutes. Soon, he will bail out and go on his merry way.

These changes were made possible by the work of two hours within a beautiful fall morning, the day America lost its compass and its wits — the day when the Post-911 World was created through bloodshed and fear.

Epilog:
747 Charter to Iraq

Just before the start of the Iraq War, in February 2003, I got a call at four in the morning from our company's crew scheduling department. My assignment was to fly a military charter, a 747 full of Camp Pendleton Marines, from San Francisco to Frankfurt, Germany, and, after a 20-hour layover, on to Kuwait. The buildup to war was being set up by the hawks in Washington; the majority of Americans somehow believed that Saddam Hussein was behind 911. In his State of the Union Address just the month before, the president had made a number of extraordinary statements. It may seem redundant to some to look back at them now, but I think even the well-informed reader may be surprised at the sheer scale and relentlessness of the deception and scare mongering that was embodied in just one speech:

> The United Nations concluded in 1999 that *Saddam Hussein had biological weapons materials sufficient to produce over 25,000 liters of anthrax; enough doses to kill several million people.*
> The United Nations concluded that *Saddam Hussein had materials sufficient to produce more than 38,000 liters of botulinum toxin; enough to subject millions of people to death by respiratory failure.*
> Our intelligence officials estimate that *Saddam Hussein had the materials to produce as much as 500 tons of sarin, mustard and VX nerve agent*. In such quantities, these chemical agents could also *kill untold thousands.*
> U.S. intelligence indicates that Saddam Hussein had *upwards of 30,000 munitions capable of delivering chemical agents.* Inspectors recently turned up 16 of them, despite Iraq's recent declaration denying their existence. Saddam Hussein *has not accounted for the remaining 29,984 of these prohibited munitions.*
> From three Iraqi defectors we know that Iraq, in the late 1990s, had *several mobile biological weapons labs*. These are designed to produce *germ warfare agents* and can be moved

from place to a place to evade inspectors. Saddam Hussein has not disclosed these facilities.

The International Atomic Energy Agency confirmed in the 1990s that *Saddam Hussein had an advanced nuclear weapons development program, had a design for a nuclear weapon and was working on five different methods of enriching uranium for a bomb.*

The British government has learned that *Saddam Hussein recently sought significant quantities of uranium from Africa.*

Our intelligence sources tell us that he has attempted to purchase *high-strength aluminum tubes suitable for nuclear weapons production.*

Saddam Hussein has not credibly explained these activities. *He clearly has much to hide.*

The dictator of Iraq is not disarming. To the contrary, *he is deceiving.*

....

Year after year, Saddam Hussein has gone to elaborate lengths, spent enormous sums, taken great risks to *build and keep weapons of mass destruction.* But why?

The only possible explanation, the only possible use he could have for those weapons, is to *dominate, intimidate or attack.*

With *nuclear arms or a full arsenal of chemical and biological weapons,* Saddam Hussein could resume his ambitions of conquest in the Middle East and create deadly havoc in that region.

And this Congress and the American people must recognize another threat. Evidence from intelligence sources, secret communications and statements by people now in custody reveal that *Saddam Hussein aids and protects terrorists, including members of Al Qaida. Secretly, and without fingerprints, he could provide one of his hidden weapons to terrorists, or help them develop their own.*

Before September the 11th, many in the world believed that Saddam Hussein could be contained. *But chemical agents, lethal viruses and shadowy terrorist networks are not easily contained.*

Imagine those 19 hijackers with other weapons and other plans, this time armed by Saddam Hussein. It would take one vial, one canister, one crate slipped into this country to bring a day of horror like none we have ever known.

We will do everything in our power to make sure that that day never comes.

Some have said we must not act until the threat is imminent.

Since when have terrorists and tyrants announced their intentions, politely putting us on notice before they strike?

If this threat is permitted to fully and suddenly emerge, all actions, all words and all recriminations would come too late.

....

And tonight I have a message for the brave and oppressed people of Iraq: Your enemy is not surrounding your country, your enemy is ruling your country.

And the day he and his regime are removed from power will be the *day of your liberation.*

The world has waited 12 years for Iraq to disarm. America will not accept a serious and mounting threat to our country and our friends and our allies.

The United States will ask the U.N. Security Council to convene on February the 5th to consider the facts of Iraq's ongoing defiance of the world. *Secretary of State Powell will present information and intelligence about Iraqi's — Iraq's illegal weapons programs, its attempts to hide those weapons from inspectors and its links to terrorist groups.*

We will consult, but let there be no misunderstanding: If Saddam Hussein does not fully disarm for the safety of our people, and for the peace of the world, we will lead a coalition to disarm him.

Tonight I have a message for the men and women who will keep the peace, members of the American armed forces. Many of you are assembling in or near the Middle East, and some crucial hours may lay ahead.

In those hours, the success of our cause will depend on you. Your training has prepared you. Your honor will guide you. *You believe in America* and America believes in you.

Sending Americans into battle is the most profound decision a president can make. The technologies of war have changed. The risks and suffering of war have not.

For the brave Americans who bear the risk, no victory is free from sorrow.

This nation fights reluctantly, because we know the cost, and we dread the days of mourning that always come.

We seek peace. We strive for peace. And sometimes peace must be defended. A future lived at the mercy of terrible threats is no peace at all.

If war is forced upon us, we will fight in a just cause and by just means, sparing, in every way we can, the innocent.

And if war is forced upon us, we will fight with the full force and might of the United States military, and we will prevail.

We had two basic choices as Americans: Either count ourselves as weak-kneed hippies or storm into Iraq and stop the nuclear holocaust Saddam was planning as an encore to 911. "You're either for us or against us" was the cry from the White House.

From my hotel room in Frankfurt I watched, between the saber-rattling and "hopes" to avoid a war, a CNN report about gunfire from a mysterious sniper at the Kuwait airport. The report was aired all day long around the world on CNN International. As the flightcrew was briefed, the sniper report was one of many concerns.

The flight was a memorable one. Our route had been altered to fly east of Iraq and to approach Kuwait from the south. We loaded our Marines and launched for a scenic trip over the Alps, down the Italian boot, over the Mediterranean, over the Sahara as the sun set, across Egypt and the Red Sea before approaching Kuwait from over the Persian Gulf. We had invited the Marines into the cockpit and enjoyed a constant stream of visitors, men and women from all over America who were being sent to establish pre-war electronic communications. Most of them were in their twenties.

Each soldier was physically fit, courteous and respectful and there was a subtle display of high confidence and intelligence. But it was an innocence in the young faces that has remained with me throughout this conflict. They were all under the distinct impression that they would take care of business in the desert and be back home within two, maybe four weeks, tops. It was very clear that a long stay in Iraq would be a disaster for them and their families. These impressive men and women were so full of life as they headed into the unknown with American flags stitched on their shoulders. These Marines believed in themselves and in the leaders who had sent them. They were proud and one thing was evident: They were eager to perform what they had been trained to do, and would rather be here on the way to battle, to defend the United States of America, than anywhere else on earth.

Most were interested in the jumbo 747-400's cockpit and

asked intelligent questions about its state-of-the-art communications and navigation systems. Passing over Rome and Mt. Vesuvius, there were five or six heads moving around to get the unique view from the monster flight deck windows. Each Marine would make sure that the next could get a view and politely rotated out of the prime positions to allow enough time for the next person to get a moment. There was mild joking and bursts of wonderment as we jetted south. The flight attendants were wearing desert fatigue hats and taking pictures of the Marines as they came through.

Personally, I had all kinds of conflicting feelings as I spoke to these men and women, looking into their clear eyes and realizing just how dedicated they were. On my days off before this trip, it happened that I had been researching the military record of their Commander-in-Chief. Details of his service, or the absence of it, have now been discussed thousands of times, but it seemed twisted that these fine soldiers were to fight under this particular president. Somewhere in the flight, one of the Marines made an ironic comment about his unit that stuck with me: "First to go, last to know."

Descending through 18,000 feet, we turned off all navigation lights and had the soldiers pull down their window shades to make the jumbo jet invisible to possible missile operators. We touched down in the desert and taxied to the military ramp on the north end of Kuwait International. I was amazed to see that our Boeing 747-400 was one of a dozen jumbo jets, including three British Airways L-1011 Tristars, a Continental Boeing 777, a Northwest 747 and few other 747s from charter outfits around the world. It looked like Kennedy Airport at rush hour. There was little doubt that America had committed to fighting a major war. Throughout the landing our heads were on a swivel looking for signs of the sniper who had been reported all day on CNN International.

Flying the 747 is an alluring job. We take off from one world and seem to land in a completely different one. The plane weighs nearly one million pounds, holds 60,000 gallons of jet fuel and burns an average of one gallon per second during 14 hours of flight. The transformation seems slow, cruising over the Pacific or the North Pole below, but when the door opens at the destination, you instantly know where you are, whether it's Hong Kong, Sydney, Beijing, Seoul, Bangkok, Frankfurt, London or San Francisco.

As I unbuckled to make my way through the Business Class upper deck to the stairs leading to the main deck, there was a tension that seemed unfamiliar. Instead of seeing business suits and our usual globe-trotting executives pulling briefcases from the overheads, there were identical gray desert fatigues and the Marines pulling rifles from the bins. It was an impressive sea of American soldiers. I made my way down to the main entry door to meet whoever would be there to open it.

As the door opened, the essence of this region, and a sudden insight into the entire upcoming conflict, smacked us all in the face. The unmistakable waft of petroleum quickly invaded the cabin as if we had landed in the Permian Basin of west Texas. Instantly, my face felt like a teenager's with an oily sheen blocking my pores. The warm silky air reeked. Everyone looked around with the same expression, as if we'd all had this moment of epiphany. There was a collective groan followed by a church-like silence as the Marines made their way from the softest seats they would see in months, away from edible food and drink. Some were walking away forever from the last purely American aspect of their lives, the last little fragment of home.

I wanted to meet the security first. A Marine sergeant in a camouflaged combat helmet opened the door and saluted me. I held out my hand and received a Marine shake that felt like the man was made of stone. I followed him down to airstairs to the tarmac as the Marines swiped their identification tags to an electronic box attached to a Plymouth minivan parked at the bottom. The first two dozen Marines proceeded directly to our cargo hold, where the sergeant shouted a few inaudible grunts. The Marines charged the cargo as if it were Normandy.

They began tossing the thousand duffel bags while I asked the sergeant about the sniper.

"What sniper?"

I told him about the all-day CNN reports.

"Look," he laughed, "I'm the head of perimeter security. If there was a sniper firing at us, I would know. There has been no sniper today, or ever. The report was bullshit, just like the rest of this dumbshit mission."

He waved his arm to the bevy of activity. "It's all bullshit."

It should not have surprised me that CNN was being used to spread propaganda, and I, even after being aware for years of press manipulation, had actually fallen for it. The poor viewers back home had two choices: Believe this fascinating report of a sniper shooting away at our American troops or fly to Kuwait and ask the head of perimeter security from the U.S. Marine Corps.

An inconspicuous eighteen-wheel truck pulled up next to the airplane. Normally, the 747 takes at least 30 minutes to be unloaded. The Marines grunted and tossed and bent and lifted and within ten minutes the entire cargo bin had been loaded into the trailer as another identical, unmarked tractor-trailer pulled up beside the first one. In the span of one minute, all 400 Marines from our flight jogged up a ramp and into the trailer and the rear cargo door was pulled down. Both trucks made their way through the perimeter gate, the troop truck bumping along as if it too carried a load of duffel bags.

Some of our crew members had tears streaming down their cheeks, and I felt a monster lump in my throat. In the last seven hours we had laughed with these people and learned what was at stake for each bright face that belonged to husbands, wives, sons, daughters, mothers and fathers over 7,000 long miles to the west. I stood with the entire crew of 15 flight attendants and my three fellow aviators as we watched the red tail lights fade into a petroleum haze of desert and darkness.